Academia

A Guide to Good Practice for Academic Managers
and Leaders in Higher Education

Graeme Wilkinson

Published by Sunway University Press
An imprint of Sunway University Sdn Bhd

No. 5, Jalan Universiti
Bandar Sunway
47500 Selangor Darul Ehsan
Malaysia

press.sunway.edu.my

ISBN 978-967-5492-09-9

Perpustakaan Negara Malaysia   Cataloguing-in-Publication Data

Wilkinson, Graeme
    Managing Effectively in Academia : A Guide to Good Practice
    for Academic Managers and Leaders in Higher Education /
    Graeme Wilkinson.
    (Sunway Shorts)
    ISBN 978-967-5492-09-9
    1. Educational leadership.
    2. Universities and colleges--Administration.
    3. College administrators.
    I. Title. II. Series.
    378.1

Edited by Sarah Loh
Designed by Rachel Goh
Typeset by Helen Wong
Printed by Vinlin Press Sdn Bhd, Malaysia

Cover image: Lera Efremova/Shutterstock.com
Image used under licence from Shutterstock.com

Contents

Preface   v

1   The Higher Education Management Challenge   1

2   Herding Cats and Catching Monkeys   11

3   Managing Academic Time and Workloads   31

4   Managing Students as Business Partners   44

5   Finding and Keeping the Stellar Cats   54

6   Managing Entrepreneurially   66

7   Managing Finances   80

8   Managing Meetings and Communications   91

9   Engaging Support Services   105

10 Managing with Analytics   113

11 Decisions, Risks, and Crises   120

12 Structures, Ambitions, and Rankings   134

13 Management and Governance   153

14 Managing Disruptive Changes   161

15 Growth as Your Leitmotif   172

List of Abbreviations   174

Notes and Further Reading   174

Acknowledgements   178

Index   180

Preface

I have written this book primarily with the aim of helping academics who are undertaking management roles in higher education to become more effective. The book should also be of value to academics who hope or expect to take on management roles in the near future and would like some guidance on what good management really means in the higher education context. Being a good manager in any organisation is certainly not easy but the academic environment presents its own unique set of challenges. By learning to be more effective as an academic manager, you can make your working life more enjoyable and also contribute more towards your institution's development.

At the outset, if you are an academic manager in a university you should recognise that universities or other higher education institutions are complex organisations involved in multiple activities such as teaching, undertaking research, offering business consultancy, and managing large estates and facilities, often including residences and conference centres. They may have several thousand staff and tens of thousands of students, a significant proportion of whom may come from overseas. They may even operate on multiple campuses in more than one country. Their staff and students are mostly highly intelligent and trained to question received wisdom and critically challenge new ideas.

The academic staff generally are, or believe themselves to be, experts in their fields and consider that they are worthy of considerable respect because of that. The students, who usually invest considerable quantities of time and money in their higher education, increasingly see themselves as "customers" and they expect high-quality service and a valuable qualification at the end of their studies as a passport to future success and wealth.

The contemporary university is thus an extremely demanding environment in which to be a manager. Not only that, but many people who find themselves in management roles in universities did not start out with a management career in mind and had not taken any significant steps to prepare themselves for it before becoming a manager. The route to becoming an academic manager is normally through being a good academic, being promoted because of it, and then being entrusted to manage people. Yet a good university teacher or researcher is not necessarily a good manager of people, at least not without some preparation or training for the role.

Lack of good management capability in universities is a refrain heard from many governments in both developed and developing countries. Governments throughout the world know full well that their universities are vital to their economic prosperity and that they need to be managed extremely well, but they also know that there are weaknesses. Some governments have put in place national training programmes for university managers, although these are, by and large, only taken up by a small proportion of the managers in the sector.

This book is focused on the role of academic managers who may lead research teams, departments, or faculties. We begin with considering what is good managerial practice, how to behave in order to be a good team leader, and what you need to understand about managing such complex institutions. We then progress to some of the broader aspects of institutional development and strategy and the individual manager's role in regard to that.

The early chapters aim to provide common-sense advice that academic managers at all levels can relate to, focusing on general day-to-day management issues such as human resource management and finance, as well as the importance of engaging effectively with non-academic support services. Much of what is written here is simply good management practice put into the context of the highly challenging university environment.

The book is intended to provide helpful practical advice to academic managers with the aim of improving organisational effectiveness. Although it has been written with new managers or newly promoted managers particularly in mind, it should be of value to anyone undertaking a management role in a university either new or long in post.

The book aims to be thought-provoking and reflective and to highlight some of the unexpected challenges that managers in universities might encounter as well as things that can and do go wrong in trying to manage universities. Also, it aims to give a perspective on governance and long-term strategic issues that managers at all levels ought to be aware of.

Many readers, myself included, may have experienced appalling managers in universities who seem capable of doing everything possible to demotivate and alienate staff and students. If this book helps to correct some of the deviant managerial behaviours that are still prevalent in many universities today, it will be a success. If, in addition, it helps already effective academic managers hone their skills and achieve new heights of managerial performance, it should help *good* universities become *great* universities.

No book on university management can ever cover every aspect of managing an institution as sophisticated and complex as a 21st-century university. It has therefore been necessary to focus on some of the key managerial topics that I personally consider to be the most important in fostering institutional effectiveness. It is an eclectic collection of topics and personal reflections, but one that I hope most readers will find appropriate and relevant to their daily lives as managers in higher education.

Management is sometimes considered to be both a science and an art. Certainly, some aspects of university management can be analysed scientifically, but most day-to-day management is about handling people and situations in order to move a highly complex organisation forward in a harmonious way to reach new levels of achievement. This, in a nutshell, is mainly an art. So, let me welcome you to the art of effective university management.

Graeme Wilkinson
Centre for Higher Education Research &
Vice-Chancellor's Office
Sunway University

CHAPTER 1

The Higher Education Management Challenge

The Higher Education Industry

The higher education "industry" is growing rapidly. Across the globe young people with ability and drive increasingly recognise that to maximise their opportunities in life they need to gain higher education qualifications. As a consequence, the higher education industry has evolved over time in most countries from what used to be a system of "elite" higher education with restricted access to a system of "mass" higher education, and then to a system of "universal" higher education in which a majority of the population undertake higher education studies at some point in their lives.

Higher education participation rates for high school-leavers are now approaching 50% in many developed countries; exceeding this in some. Data from the Office of National Statistics, United Kingdom (UK) show that in some parts of Greater London, the proportion of the 16-to-64-year-old population with degrees exceeds 50%

and in one borough—the City of London—it has passed 70%. Although in most developing countries the trend is towards a mass system, with a universal system some way off, growth is accelerating.

Higher education is, therefore, a truly global expanding industry. At the height of the western financial crisis in 2008, the London head of a global investment bank was asked which industry he thought gave the most hope for economic recovery. His answer, surprisingly for many, was "higher education". Higher education catalyses economic development and universities are themselves major employers. In some small cities, they may even be the largest employer overall.

As the demand for higher education has been growing, national higher education systems have become enormous and increasingly complex with many challenges particularly related to resourcing.[1,2] The expansion of state-funded universities has been rapid in many countries. However, governments have increasingly had to turn to the students themselves to fund the cost through higher fees or graduate taxes. They also look to international students to bring in additional revenue through paying higher fees than domestic students.

In some countries, governments have reached the limit of what they can realistically afford and have been looking to the private sector to fill the gap. The growth rate of private higher education is now well ahead of the growth rate in state-funded higher education globally.

This is a trend that is likely to continue in the coming decades. The demand is such that students and their families are increasingly willing to pay privately for what their governments may not be able to provide publicly.

There are currently in excess of 30,000 higher education institutions in the world, based on the biannual Webometrics ranking. Not all have the label of "university", but they nonetheless provide higher qualifications such as diplomas and degrees. To function effectively and deliver what their "customers" want, these institutions need to be managed well. They offer a sophisticated "product" to a highly intelligent, discerning, and demanding multicultural clientele.

Students want the qualifications and higher-level professional skills that will give them success in their careers and enable them to meet their personal life goals and ambitions. When so much is at stake, students will naturally expect to receive very good service and a high-quality outcome from their university experience. Governments and companies that fund research at universities also want good returns for their investment.

It is an undeniable fact that universities, once regarded as rarefied "ivory towers", are now powerhouses of economic activity of great importance to nations. They have great value to their students and to society, and they drive innovation.[2] Good management is essential for such institutions to function effectively and to deliver what everyone wants. Yet universities are not institutions

3

that were once thought to require "management". They originated in medieval times as tranquil monastic communities of scholars in which the concept of *management* as we know it today probably would not have been understood.

Many distinguished universities still retain ancient traditions and modes of behaviour that do not sit comfortably with modern methods of industrial management. However, given the scale of the industry and the size of most university-level institutions as well as the demands placed on them by society, professional high-quality management is now obligatory.

> **Universities, once regarded as rarefied "ivory towers", are now powerhouses of economic activity of great importance to nations.**

Academics in positions of responsibility, such as heads or chairs of departments or deans, have to see themselves primarily as managers of people and other resources. Their roles as academic specialists might even become secondary. This is something that can come as a surprise to a newly elected or promoted academic department head who, up until that time, spent most of his or her time focusing on being a good researcher or teacher.

Managing in Higher Education

Universities present particularly interesting challenges to any manager, and particularly to new managers. They are enormously complex organisations and becoming more so as time goes by.[3] They are also evolving very fast with new types of international partnerships, for example, forging new pathways for institutional development.[4] The fast pace of development is global, but in Asia there is a strong focus on learning how to develop high-quality institutions rapidly[5] and taking on the longer-established institutions in the West in a global competition for academic supremacy.

Interestingly, most textbooks written on the subject of management are in fact written by university academics who are usually thinking about industries other than their own. Yet their own is one of the most interesting and challenging ones in which to be a manager.

Universities tend to be medium- to large-sized organisations. Most range from having a few hundred to a few thousand staff. There are no mega-corporations in the university world, nor are there small enterprises, with very few exceptions. Their main "customers"—the students—typically turn up on-site almost every day for a period of several years, even though there is a trend towards more online delivery. (We shall look at the notion of students as customers more closely later.)

Academics have to multitask and divide their time between supporting their increasingly demanding students and fulfilling other roles, such as undertaking research and consultancy work. In the banking industry, this would be similar to investment analysts also advising customers in a retail branch—an almost unthinkable idea. Increasingly, academics find themselves doing a lot of unwelcome bureaucratic work in addition, much of it required by statutory bodies.

Another special dimension of universities is the separation between the academic functions and the support service functions. Usually, the numbers of staff are split roughly equally between the two types of function in totality, though the academic functions have much greater visibility to the outside world. Academic staff have a natural tendency to think of themselves as performing the core business of the institution and undertaking the bulk of the customer-facing activity, but this is not necessarily so.

A further peculiarity of universities, as organisations, is the division into subject disciplines all performing broadly the same tasks, such as teaching and research, but in different ways. Lack of standardisation of processes and procedures is a real issue for many universities where academic departments become insular, operating as mini fiefdoms.

Academics like to do things their own way and any attempts to enforce consistency and standard operating procedures can be met with resistance. From my personal experience, the more exalted the university, the greater this tendency appears to be.

Managing effectively in a university means managing competently as in any other type of organisation, while adapting to the special nature of the higher education industry and its key stakeholders. It has often been said that trying to manage academics is like trying to herd cats.[6] While there may be some element of truth in this, the reality is that academics are professionals doing an important job in a demanding context and they do appreciate being sensibly and competently managed and indeed, expect this.

Everyone wants their managers to have a clear vision of where the organisation is going. They also want their managers to be competent in managing people and resources to get there. A university is no different from any other type of business or public-sector organisation in this regard. The cats are amenable to being herded if treated well.

It is not the purpose of this book to serve just as a management primer—there are plenty of other books that do that. The main purpose of this book is to provide insight into the special issues pertaining to

> **It has often been said that trying to manage academics is like trying to herd cats...The cats are amenable to being herded if treated well.**

university management for those who find themselves in academic managerial roles often without any prior training or clear appreciation of what such roles entail.

Being an effective manager in a university is potentially very rewarding. Managers usually have more freedom than the people they manage and often enjoy a salary premium. Academics with managerial responsibilities typically have lower teaching loads. If they are prepared well for their roles, and thereby become comfortable with them, their jobs can be relatively enjoyable. It is also true that universities very rarely close. Mergers sometimes happen, but rarely outright closures.

Even though the fortunes of universities can wax and wane, it is rare for any university to have to declare significant numbers of staff redundancies. Managers in universities are therefore normally spared some of the more challenging and unpleasant situations in other industries where whole companies or divisions may be completely eliminated in a short period of time due to new competitors or declining markets for obsolete products, or lack of innovation in the face of disruptive innovation by new players in the market.

Even the advent of massive open online courses (MOOCs), though often portrayed by advocates as a disruptive technology in the higher education field, is unlikely to undermine rapidly the core business of most universities. The jury is still out on this long-term, but in the short to medium term most universities do not feel threatened by MOOCs, seeing them as an opportunity rather than a threat. We shall return to this and the broader issue of disruptive change later.

Undertaking a management role in a university can, in some respects, be a less worrisome or less stressful role than undertaking such a role in other industries, though many academic managers might not necessarily agree with this. This may be because those who undertake such roles have often arrived in them primarily because of demonstrated academic ability and they might lack adequate training.

With the right training on good management practice and an excellent insight into the issues that confront universities and how to deal with them, being a manager in a university can be a thoroughly enjoyable job. Good management practice in universities is so important, not only because of the health of the organisation overall but because it impacts on the lives of so many people: the staff members and the students who probably outnumber the staff by at least a factor of 10:1 (and commonly by much more than that).

In the chapters that follow, we shall examine some of the key issues regarding good management in a higher education institution. There are many aspects to university management, but fundamentally they mostly relate to:

- Managing staff and "star" academics
- Managing students, parents, and other stakeholders
- Managing finances and other important resources

- Managing development
- Managing change
- Managing communications, and handling complex decisions
- Managing ambition and reputation
- Managing disruptive innovations
- Managing governance

We shall cover these as well as some of the related challenges such as managing risks and crises in the book.

Some readers may wonder why the emphasis is on *management* rather than *leadership*. It is an interesting question as to whether management or leadership is the most important and how these two rather broad terms are related, if at all. This book is written from the standpoint that universities require their most senior staff to work highly effectively to take the institution forward and to deliver high-quality service to their stakeholders.

Whether working effectively as a senior member of the institution is described as management or leadership, or both, is less important than actually doing it and ensuring the best outcomes for everyone involved. We shall focus on behaviour modes linked to good outcomes without trying to differentiate leadership from management, with apologies to the many academics around the world in business schools who spend a lot of time researching, thinking, and writing about these two concepts.

CHAPTER 2

Herding Cats and Catching Monkeys

The Challenge of Managing People

There are many dimensions to management in universities, but they are all concerned in one way or another with managing resources optimally to achieve an institution's current goals and longer-term strategic objectives. Of all the resources that have to be managed, the most important by far for any manager is his or her team of people. Other resources such as buildings, plant, finances, etc., do require careful management, but they are usually nowhere near as complicated as managing people.

In this chapter, we shall review the basics of good people management as they apply in universities. For any academic manager in a university, especially a novice manager, mastering the management of people is a fundamental requirement for creating a strong team that helps to build a dynamic, high-quality institution. Some of what follows may be familiar to readers who have had

11

some basic management training. What follows is my attempt to help you "herd" the cats.

There are many theories about what employees want from their work and their lives and how managers need to satisfy their requirements in order to motivate them. Abraham Maslow's famous hierarchy of needs theory describes how at the most fundamental level people need their physiological needs satisfied. They then need safety and security, a sense of being loved and belonging, and a feeling of esteem and respect until they reach the top of the hierarchy where, if all other needs below have been satisfied, they want self-actualisation, or the capacity to be creative, spontaneous and to solve problems.

Managers need to strive to manage in such a way that their employees' needs are satisfied all the way up through the hierarchy if they want a satisfied and fulfilled team. Employees who are given the freedom and flexibility to self-actualise will be well motivated. In a university context, the need for self-actualisation is particularly strong because academics thrive on being creative deep thinkers with an independent spirit.

One of the first things a manager in a university, whether new or experienced, needs to recognise is that he or she needs to build a high-performing team, whatever it is or however large that team might be. There are well-known approaches for doing that.[7] Secondly, his or her team members have human needs like any other individuals on the planet. They need to be respected as colleagues and

12

not regarded as "inferiors" or "subordinates". They are people who have an important contribution to make and on whom the institution depends to achieve its goals.

The fundamental truth that all higher education managers need to understand is that no one wants, or likes, to be "managed". This applies in universities as in any other work context. No human being wants another human being to tell him or her what to do, when to do it, or how to do it. Neither do they want to be directed to achieve certain pre-defined goals or to follow specific plans. Indeed, many traditional approaches to management such as management by objectives are now questioned by contemporary thinkers and researchers on talent management.[8]

Academics, in particular, have a strong aversion to being directed. They have been brought up to think of themselves as experts in their field. No one who considers himself or herself to be an expert takes easily to the idea that someone else may wish to direct what he or she does. Hence, the role of a manager in a university is a particularly difficult one requiring considerable skills of tact and diplomacy.

> **Academics prefer not to be managed and usually consider that they are so intelligent that they do not need to be.**

Thus, in trying to manage people, an academic manager needs to recognise that the people who report to him or her, especially academics, would prefer not to be managed and usually consider that they are so intelligent that they do not need to be. The strength of that feeling can depend on many factors which will be explored later. If you really want to be a successful university manager the first requirement is for you to be aware of this aversion of staff members to being managed.

Use of Emotional Intelligence

One of the most important aspects of management in higher education is the use of emotional intelligence (EI). The concept of EI was introduced by psychologists Peter Salovey (now President of Yale University) and John Mayer in the 1980s. Good managers are essentially managers who are well able to use their own emotions and their understanding of the emotions of others in their daily management activities. They use EI and have a strong emotional intelligence quotient (EQ).

The key skills for using EI in management have been well documented by Salovey and David Caruso.[9] Emotionally intelligent managers use their emotions and those of others in making good business decisions. The emotions and emotional reactions are seen as important parameters that can and should be used to inform decision-making.

Interestingly, although universities are full of highly intelligent individuals in the intelligence quotient (IQ) sense, such individuals are sometimes not emotionally intelligent. Some seem to possess high IQ, but rather less EQ. It is indeed quite common to find individuals promoted into management positions in universities because of their undoubted academic ability and capacity to drive research or academic programmes. Academics who have shown the capacity to undertake high-quality research and write well for international journals can often be prioritised in promotion rounds and eventually begin to become managers of people. Writing for top-ranked international academic journals, however, requires no EI.

The lack of EI can be a real handicap for a university manager. He or she can come over as insensitive, distant, arrogant, or uncaring. It is important that any manager in a university is able to communicate effectively with his or her staff and motivate them. To do this effectively requires a good appreciation of their emotional state and feelings, which also means being empathetic.

The model of EI developed by Salovey and his colleagues is based on four key skills: identifying and becoming aware of emotions, using emotions and letting them influence thinking, understanding emotions, and managing emotions including integrating them into thinking about management issues. Effective organisational management requires the use of such skills.

There are many situations in universities where good application of the four skills of emotional management can yield significant advantages. Academic staff are most comfortable with consultative management styles. As intelligent people themselves, they expect to be able to share their views on management decisions. Often their views will be moderated by their emotional response to particular situations.

It is imperative therefore for a university manager to understand the emotional aspects of particular situations. Failure to do so will appear as a failure to effectively understand the feelings of the staff, which will appear highly non-consultative. If I could point to one fundamental error which some academic managers make that derails their careers and leads to dysfunctional departments, it is the failure to use EI. If you are now managing a team in a university, one of the main things to think about is whether you are personally making full use of EI and whether your staff perceive you as empathetic.

University managers who take seemingly logical management decisions based on cold analysis of the situation using their IQ without considering the EI dimensions will not be perceived as good managers. This can ultimately lead to poor management style and even the removal of the manager from his or her role if the balance is not shifted back towards a combined use of IQ and EQ.

University staff respond well to an emotionally intelligent management style and a good manager will use his or her EI effectively. Not only that, but managers seeking promotion to the highest levels of senior management in universities should make it a priority to develop their EI skills accordingly. Taking this aspect of personal development seriously is as important as developing skills and knowledge in academic areas and technical areas relevant to management such as in financial management.

It is, of course, interesting to consider the cultural context for using EI. There are some cultures, for example in Asia, where there may be reluctance either to show or to use emotions. This may be seen as a sign of weakness in highly hierarchical and meritocratic structures, but for universities

One fundamental error which some academic managers make that leads to dysfunctional departments is the failure to use EI.

to blossom, there is little doubt that their managers should embrace the use of EI, even if this can pose some cultural challenges.

Vision, Delegation, and Coaching

Fundamentally, to be a good manager, you must in the first instance communicate a clear vision of where your organisation is going and what your team's role will be in helping it get there. Everyone wants to feel a sense of belonging to something with a purpose and a future. No one wants to feel themselves to be part of a dead-end, moribund university with no vision. Normally, the vision for the organisation is something that is communicated by senior management, normally the vice-chancellor or president.

Once the vision has been established, the role of a manager in the institution is to ensure that his or her team understands that vision and that team members know what they have to do to help make that vision a reality. Their role may only contribute in a very small way to the achievement of the corporate vision, but nonetheless, they must feel they are part of it. This means they need to be reminded on a regular basis of what the vision is and how they are working towards it. This does not mean that they need to be told every day about the corporate vision, but they should be subtly reminded about how the institution is doing and how their efforts are helping to achieve the big picture in the long term.

More precisely, a manager's role is to translate the corporate vision into the objectives of the team and then to help the team determine and carry out the actions required. Good management is all about that. It is concerned with translating the corporate vision and goals into objectives and specific actions that a team needs to carry out.

For a team to work effectively, it needs to understand the overarching vision and then understand its own priorities as a team in helping to achieve the vision. When it comes to determining the actions to be carried out, a high degree of self-determination is necessary so that team members feel valued and are able to work out for themselves, as much as possible, how they will help to realise ultimately the corporate vision. A team that works it all out for itself is much more likely to be committed to realising the overall vision than one that is told in minute detail precisely what to do. This is essentially the empowerment of a team and it works well in academia.

Another key aspect of good management in a university context, indeed in any organisational context, is delegation. Good delegation involves distributing tasks and allowing staff to take full responsibility for them and, most importantly, allowing them to undertake the tasks in the way that they determine. This is a very good management practice and it works well in universities because very bright people, who desire self-actualisation, usually enjoy challenges and taking responsibility for significant projects or tasks.

A typical example might be a department head delegating the writing of the curriculum for a new degree programme to a more junior academic, or a senior professor delegating the writing of a research grant proposal to a more junior research fellow. In both such examples, the delegated member of staff is likely to find the project demanding but enjoyable and developmental in regard to their own careers.

However, it is also necessary to issue a word of caution regarding delegation. Tasks should not be delegated that are more naturally the manager's own and which are particularly unpleasant or difficult to carry out. Managers who appear to want to avoid difficult or unpleasant tasks and are using their power and position in the institution to dump these tasks on others can soon lose the respect of their staff by doing that. Furthermore, academics want to take responsibility for their own contributions and do not want to get diverted by taking on difficult tasks passed down from someone else.

Delegating too much can get in the way of staff taking their own initiatives, biasing their work towards the priorities of a manager instead of their own. So, delegation is good, but up to a point. Being guided by EI helps you to avoid inappropriate delegation. Once tasks have been delegated, it is then good practice for you as a manager to support staff in carrying them out, not as a "boss" but as a "coach".

The term "coaching" describes pretty accurately what a good manager should be doing. Thinking like a "coach" and not a "boss" is something good university managers should do at all times. It really does not matter what level a manager is at in an institution, nor how many reporting staff he or she is leading. Managers who act as a coach to those who report to them will normally get good performance from them. Managers who act as coaches are supporters, mentors, encouragers, facilitators, and rewarders. Those who do not act like this can be viewed as dictators, instruction givers, rule givers, or punishers—all of which are definitely not appreciated in academia.

Managers in any industry get the best from their teams when they behave as though they and their teams are in a tough competition and are working together to win. Every person has their role to play in that game, and the role of the manager is to help facilitate the game plan and to work with the team to implement it. The game may, for example, be one of aiming to become a leading department in a particular academic subject area in the world.

Objective Setting

It is sometimes said that for an organisation to be effective, every team and every individual needs to have SMART—specific, measurable, achievable, realistic, and timed—objectives. Some organisations go out of their way to ensure that the entire organisation is managed by setting detailed specifications of objectives for each employee and working out timescales for their achievement and measuring the outcomes.

While this may work in some contexts, few organisations can function like this in reality. The SMART approach implies that the work of each employee can be programmed like the instructions to be performed in a piece of software. This mechanistic view of an organisation is often far from reality and particularly so in higher education because academics like to be driven by their own intellectual curiosity, which is incompatible with a programmed task-based approach to work management.

Moreover, things change so fast in academia that setting goals can be a bit like deciding where to drive by only looking in the rear-view mirror. You know how you got to where you are today and think that will be sufficient to guide you forward, but it usually is not and the road ahead changes as you move along it.

However, having said that, institutions do often need to set some targets for staff to achieve, such as producing a certain number of research publications per year or attracting a certain amount of grant income to meet top-level institutional objectives. This dichotomy between achieving top-level institutional objectives on the one hand, and allowing freedom and independent thinking on the other, can lead to tension in the academic context and put you as a manager in a delicate position of trying to strike an appropriate balance between the two things.

Another management practice that I would encourage in the university context is sometimes called "management by walking around" or MBWA. Essentially this means getting out of the office, walking around to see what is going on, and interacting with staff. Given the unfortunate tendency these days for people to manage by messaging systems such as WhatsApp or by email, moving around campus to talk to people needs to be given a higher priority. You do not need to do this all the time, but you should make a habit of wandering around the campus regularly and chatting to people informally. It is sometimes all too easy to hide in a laboratory or office and ignore what is actually happening around you.

It is, of course, important for university managers to have regular meetings with their teams to review how things are going. Meetings are an avenue to discuss ideas for new priorities and new actions as well as how to respond to unexpected events. Sometimes these may need to be formal and recorded in minutes, especially if there is a need to report to a higher authority on progress of particular projects or if a report has to be submitted to external agencies, partners, clients, or regulatory bodies.

The best type of team meetings, however, are informal ones where the manager and the team sit down to discuss issues as collaborative problem-solvers, throwing ideas around, brainstorming solutions to problems, etc. The manager might be the chair of such meetings, but fundamentally, these meetings need to be ones where each member has an equal voice. Team meetings are an important part of communication in universities. In my experience, staff engagement in universities suffers considerably when teams do not meet and academic managers spend too little time communicating with their staff.

Catching "Monkeys"

Let us now turn to one other challenge that any good university manager needs to look out for in handling people. Occasionally, managers find that there are individuals within their staff who will try to pass tasks up to them. Something will arise that needs looking into or dealing with and they will suggest the manager should take it on.

Usually, these will be small but irritating tasks that do not seem to fit anyone's particular job role and the people passing them upwards do not know how to handle them. Effectively, it is delegation in reverse because the task is "delegated" by the staff member upwards to their manager rather than downwards as in normal delegation. It is all too easy for inexperienced academic managers to acquiesce.

A typical scenario may go like this: An academic staff member who directs a particular programme passes his department head in the corridor and tells his head that his students are complaining that the campus bus service is too irregular and needs to be improved. He asks the head to intervene and deal with it. This is clearly a case where the head could deal with it if he or she felt like it.

The campus bus service, however, is not the head's responsibility; it is actually managed by the campus facilities department. The programme director could easily call or email the campus facilities department to pass on the concern of his students. He does not need his department head to do it, but effectively in the short corridor encounter, the programme director has passed the issue up to his head and washed his hands of it.

It is not a problem if this happens infrequently, but if the department head has many encounters like this in a typical working day, it is easy to accumulate so many issues to resolve that he or she can no longer focus on key tasks and objectives. Effectively his or her time is all taken up in handling such issues.

It can become quite easy for managers to collect numerous mini-tasks or issues to resolve and managers can end up having their daily workload dictated by their staff. This is sometimes referred to as "passing the monkey".[10] Good managers in universities do not need their staff passing them many monkeys, especially ones that do not necessarily require someone in their position to act.

When it is suggested that a manager should do something for an individual or for the team as a whole, the manager should try to identify if it is a case of monkey passing. Ideally, the manager wants the team to deal with all monkeys themselves. They need to learn how to deal with unusual or tricky issues that come up without passing them upwards.

By taking on unusual challenges or dealing with unexpected problems, teams will grow in their own confidence. A manager needs to recognise the monkeys for what they are, *catch* them, and pass them back. Monkey catching is not just about keeping a manager's own workload and schedule under control, it is also about enabling staff to develop as problem solvers. As an academic manager, you want to achieve both objectives.

> **Monkey catching enables staff to develop as problem solvers.**

Arguably, one of the biggest sources of monkeys in academia is committees. When a group of people sit around a table to discuss issues, they can soon come up with all kinds of tasks that need to be carried out; some of high priority, some of much lower priority. All tasks nonetheless end up as actions to be followed up by someone and often get passed to a manager to look at by decision of the committee. More often than not, these are monkeys and they can seriously disrupt a manager's personal work priorities. We will talk more about university committees in Chapter 8, but considering them as monkey-generating machines is not too far wrong!

Managing Poor Performance

So far in this chapter, we have examined what a manager has to do to make his or her team feel valued and perform well. It is also worth considering what happens when sometimes university managers have to deal with bad behaviour or poor performance. This should not happen too frequently if they have put in place a well-chosen team and have managed the team well as a coach so that the team can learn to grow and thrive under their guidance and mentorship.

Yet sometimes you will undoubtedly have to deal with some poor performers. Dealing with poor performance is necessary in order not to demotivate an academic team as a whole. If a team sees one member getting away with poor performance, there can be a feeling that the whole team is being dragged down or its reputation damaged. Others may begin to wonder why they should work hard and strive for the betterment of the university if others can get away with doing very little or doing it badly.

There are whole textbooks written about how to deal with bad behaviour, performance, or attitude in the workplace, but I have one simple message in such cases. There may come a point at which a manager will have to give a member of staff a formal warning or instigate a disciplinary process which could even end in dismissal. However, it is far better to avoid getting to that stage if at all possible. If a member of staff is starting to show signs of poor performance, the manager should try to deal with it one-to-one informally in the first instance, communicating clearly and unambiguously about his or her concern. The manager might want to probe to find out what is really causing the performance issue.

Quite often poor performance at work is a result of problems elsewhere, such as at home. Perhaps the individual is undergoing a marriage breakdown or something like that. Good managers should try to treat the individual concerned as a human with human needs, requirements, and problems. They should aim to get underneath the problems and help the individual seek out help as necessary.

Of course, there may be other reasons for poor performance that a manager can help to overcome. Maybe the individual finds someone else in the team a problem or maybe there is a lack of a certain resource required. Maybe the individual lacks some specific knowledge and needs some training. Managers should aim to be good listeners, identify the causes of problems if they can, and then do something to help, always using EI as part of the process.

It is rare for workers to be deliberately lazy at work, or to deliberately undermine the success of the organisation, especially in a university where academics will have proven their ability to work hard through having overcome many academic hurdles to qualify for their jobs in the first place. If academics are managed appropriately and are well-motivated they are not normally lazy, but if anyone is showing tendencies in this direction managers can encourage corrective behaviour by team pressure. When academic teams meet to discuss progress on activities and projects, anyone who has not been performing will be embarrassed by having little to report in front of their colleagues. Peer pressure will force them to have more to report next time.

Sometimes the manager can intervene in a subtle way, behind the scenes, to encourage another team member to speak to someone who is performing poorly. Individuals may respond more favourably to a colleague in their own team than their manager approaching them to find out why there is a problem with their behaviour or work attitude. Managers, even good ones, may sometimes be perceived as unapproachable and in difficult circumstances can be feared. It may be easier to get improved behaviour through one-to-one peer approaches that the manager can initiate.

Managing Upwards

This chapter would not be complete without some consideration of how to manage upwards effectively. Every manager in a university has to report upwards, including the president or vice-chancellor, who will normally have to report to a governing board or one of its members. A key challenge for any manager is to manage well both downwards and upwards.

Managing downwards is all about team management, which we have already discussed. Managing downwards involves building teams that perform well and coaching them to achieve objectives that are consistent with the institutional vision and mission, and which are likely to be required by more senior managers.

Managing upwards, however, is all about handling those above you in an institutional management hierarchy. Managing upwards is about carefully interpreting the aims of more senior managers, working with them to ensure their broad objectives are met, and then feeding back to them ideas, progress reports, and views or issues from staff teams below.

Managing in both directions simultaneously can be challenging or even stressful. An academic manager can be in a difficult place, sandwiched between more senior managers and his or her staff team, acting as a go-between. The key to being a successful manager in the middle of the academic "sandwich" is to view the entire structure, from senior managers down, as a high-performing extended team. Your role is then to work towards getting the most from all parts of the structure, by communicating effectively and ensuring alignment of efforts towards the corporate vision, and solving problems if alignment is not occurring.

A common failing of inexperienced managers is to champion the interests of his or her department or unit and to ignore the broader institutional priorities set by senior managers above. By acting solely as the champion of your part of the institution, you may easily end up in conflict with your senior managers or in turf wars with other departments or units. Seeing issues holistically from an institutional level perspective is a key determinant of those managers who are ripe to become the next senior managers or institutional heads.

In conclusion, the essence of good people management in universities is for managers to set and communicate a clear vision and sense of direction, use EI, manage like a team coach, ensure staff establish clear priorities for themselves in alignment with the vision, avoid monkey passes, always deal fairly and appropriately with poor performers, and manage upwards effectively. It is quite simple really, but surprisingly easy for a manager to get wrong—as I have witnessed on many occasions in multiple higher education institutions!

CHAPTER 3

Managing Academic Time and Workloads

The Nature of the Academic Working Day

Managing the workloads of academics is a particularly thorny issue which, in my experience, is one of the most difficult things for an academic manager to handle. I say this from the perspective of having worked as a manager in four universities; in each, the workload issue was always one that bothered academics the most.

With the advent of advanced tablet computers and smartphones, working practices are evolving throughout the world. The division between working time and leisure time is increasingly blurred. Everyone is getting used to the idea of almost 24/7 availability for phone calls, emails, tweets, WhatsApp messages, etc., for work or leisure purposes. There is simply no longer a firm boundary between work and leisure. Admittedly, most work activities take place during office hours, but increasingly many do not.

Working practices are of course changing in higher education just as in many other industries. This is partly a result of the change in teaching and learning approaches. Increasingly, university programmes are delivered through blended learning, in which formal scheduled classes are supplemented by online learning materials that can be studied whenever the student wishes.

Students now expect online support from their tutors via email or social media as well as the traditional meeting in an office. Students are now essentially living very complex lives in which study, work, leisure, and sleep are all mixed up in what for some can be a very chaotic cocktail. Their demands for educational support can come at all hours of the day. Academics are getting used to having to support them wherever and whenever, including at night.

The lives of academics are likewise becoming very chaotic. A typical academic will have to juggle the multiple demands of having to produce high-quality teaching materials, carrying out research and writing papers, conducting formal classes, assessing student work, meeting students (and sometimes parents) face-to-face, providing online teaching resources, and, of course, providing feedback and advice to students via email, internet chat, or phone at almost any time of day.

Moreover, academics will often be required to undertake course administration, support recruitment and fundraising events, and meet with employers. In addition to all this, they also have private lives and many have dependants to look after

As an academic manager, you need to be aware of the complex life patterns of students and academics and manage them accordingly. Managers need to be sensitive to the demands on academics and not to expect too much conformity to a standard nine-to-five office hours' model. You have to consider whether it is reasonable to expect academics to be on campus every day from 9 am to 5 pm if you would also like them to answer student emails on their smartphones at 10 pm in the evening when they are at home.

Academics also need a lot of quiet thinking time if they are to produce high-quality teaching materials and write high-impact journal papers. Such activities need to be done in peace and quiet. This is often not possible on a busy campus especially if the academic staff have to work in multi-occupancy offices or even open-plan offices.

In some institutions, the move towards large open-plan offices seating many academics is controversial and can lead to changes in working behaviour.[11] It can lead to greater collaboration between staff members but also reduces the opportunity for quiet study and reflection which may be critical to undertaking high-quality research and preparing teaching material.

Open-plan offices with hot-desking and end-of-day "clean desk" policies mean academics may have no regular fixed work location on campus and are unable to surround themselves with their books or other materials. As research and teaching materials are increasingly electronic, this is less of a problem than it used to be. However, many academics still want to be near their books and have a quiet space in which to work and if this is denied them on campus, they will tend to spend more time working from home.

Estate planners often fail to understand what the life of an academic involves and think that by packing more of them into larger spaces they are taking the university forward, but this is not necessarily so. The best universities provide academics with at least some quiet private spaces in which to work even if open-plan spaces are also part of the estate's mix.

Academics will often find it much easier to write a book or research paper in the comfort of their home at a time of day when they find they can best think, rather than in an office environment between 9 am and 5 pm. Managing the time of academics is thus a difficult and sensitive issue. Some universities expect or demand academic staff attendance from 9 am to 5 pm, five days a week. Absences are not permitted unless "booked" in advance. Certainly, by requiring such attendance the university can be sure that staff will always be available to see students informally as well as to conduct formal scheduled classes. Yet if a university requires adherence to a rigid timetable, is it then reasonable to expect staff also to answer student emails in the evenings and at weekends at home? Probably not.

A Results-Oriented Work Environment

More enlightened institutions, which are almost certainly the majority these days, allow academics flexibility in their attendance patterns on campus, though it is not so in all institutions and in some countries in particular. The really tricky management challenge is to work out how much flexibility to allow.

Flexibility can allow good academics to achieve great things: to produce beautifully designed teaching materials, to come up with really novel ideas in their research, and to give outstanding support to their students at unusual times of the day. On the other hand, flexibility can also allow weak academics to underperform. They may rarely show up for work on campus, except when required to teach formal classes. They may often say they are "working from home" yet produce very little and essentially enjoy becoming a part-time worker on a full-time salary.

Managing working time flexibility for academics can be one of the most significant challenges a new academic manager, such as a department head, has to face. In some world-class research institutions, it is not such a significant problem because the vast majority of the academics are driven to build their stellar research careers and most likely will be thinking about their research almost every moment they are awake.

In most institutions, however, managing academic working time is quite difficult. Some staff will use flexibility to achieve outstanding results for the university. Others

> **Managing working time flexibility for academics can be one of the most significant challenges for a new academic manager.**

will use flexibility to enjoy themselves and give little back to their institutions. Academic managers, therefore, need to find a way to use flexibility, but in a way that ensures good outcomes for the institution.

The key to this is to look at the results produced by each academic member of staff. What matters is what they produce, not when or where they do it. Managers need to judge their staff in terms of their contribution to the university. This can be assessed in many ways. Typical measures might be student satisfaction with the teaching they receive, the number of research papers published and their citation counts, the quality of student feedback on assessments, or the percentage of students achieving high grades on modules taught.

With an appropriate mechanism for evaluating the productivity and achievement of each member of staff, it is perfectly feasible to have a very relaxed attitude to attendance on campus, as long as staff turn up on time for their scheduled classes, for required team meetings, and for informal meetings with students and colleagues, which might be at fixed times of the week or informally arranged via email. This approach is what is increasingly becoming known as the "results-oriented work environment",[12,13] which advocates a complete focus on results with effectively zero attention to attendance patterns as long as the work gets done.

Academia is in many ways an ideal environment for a results-focused approach to attendance management. Academics are highly intelligent professionals who are fully capable of managing a very varied daily timetable and delivering outstanding results in a flexible way. Indeed, academics who have been trained to be creative educators and have brilliant research ideas are not people to be managed tightly in terms of their time and attendance like factory floor workers.

Any university or academic manager that tries to do so will get into conflict with staff quite quickly. Good managers will be very comfortable with granting time flexibility, provided they monitor results and deal with underperformers. Good performers who make the best of the flexibility offered to them will expect underperformers to be dealt with, otherwise, they will question why they themselves work so hard when others use flexibility to avoid doing much work.

Alongside the issue of managing academic time is determining what academics spend their time on. This will normally be a mix of teaching and research with lesser amounts of administrative, pastoral, and consulting activities added on. One of the interesting challenges in any university is to enable all academics to reach their full potential. Increasingly, as the world moves towards universal higher education, it is becoming apparent that not all academics can, or should be, top-quality researchers as well as excellent teachers.

> **Good managers will be very comfortable with granting time flexibility, provided they monitor results and deal with underperformers.**

While it is highly desirable for students to be taught by outstanding researchers who will pass on the latest ideas from their research, overall far more university "teachers" are needed in the world than "researchers". It has become a standard mantra in most institutions, fed by government agencies in many countries, that universities or similar institutions of higher learning have to undertake research as well as teaching and need to be rated on their performance in both.

Institutions that are seen only to be fulfilling solely a teaching mission do not get the full respect that they deserve. This is of course fuelled by the international university ranking systems that are focused primarily on research performance and reputation. A university that does outstanding teaching, yielding substantial levels of added value through training young people to be highly active knowledge workers, is not likely to be highly regarded unless it is also publishing many research papers and obtaining research grants. This is undoubtedly an outdated way of thinking. Universities are required to generate new knowledge, but they do not all have to do this, especially in countries with near-universal access to higher education.

Over the last two decades, there has been rapid growth in the number of research papers produced and journals publishing them. In my past experience as an associate editor of several international journals for over a decade, the number of papers submitted and published has been rising seemingly exponentially year-on-year. Yet the quality of those papers has not improved and most appear to make only minor contributions to their specific field or to the vast sum of human knowledge.

It appears, and this is very much an informed personal view, that too many academics are researching too many minor problems of little significance to humankind just to get published and to justify their existence as academics. Much duplication and investigation of trivial matters with inconsequential results are being written up for peer-reviewed publication. Peer reviewers are becoming swamped with papers and the quality of reviewing appears noticeably to be steadily declining.

Some institutions globally have chosen to implement career pathways for academics that allow them to choose between teaching and research, teaching only, or research only. Job titles such as Teaching Fellow are used as well as Lecturer or Research Fellow, depending on the individual's focus and career pathway.

By implementing such career pathways, it enables good teachers who do not want to do mediocre research to focus only on becoming excellent teachers. Enlightened institutions trying this find that it is possible to motivate strongly those staff who enjoy university teaching. With appropriate promotional routes and reward structures for excellent teachers, it is possible to create an outstanding educational environment with highly satisfied staff and students. Moreover, companies employing the graduates may be very pleased with the "product" they are getting.

Building a strong research culture also helps to build a strong teaching culture. Evidence from many assessments of university quality in a variety of countries has shown that the best research is highly correlated with the best teaching. Why is this so? There are several factors at play here. Firstly, strong research universities are generally better funded than weak research universities. Research-focused universities generally have grant income as well as consultancy income that can lead to better staff-to-student ratios.

Secondly, research-focused academics tend to operate at the frontiers of their fields, are more up-to-date on recent developments, and can build case studies from their research and consultancy work into their teaching. This is much more interesting and enjoyable from a student perspective.

Thirdly, academics with a strong focus on research are likely to have a natural tendency to explore ideas and try things out, and are used to preparing material carefully and clearly for consumption by others (e.g., as peer-reviewed journal articles) This capacity for exploration and clarity of presentation also results in the production of high-quality teaching materials.

This does not mean that academics who are not internationally recognised researchers cannot be good university teachers. Those that do become outstanding teachers, however, have to work very hard at developing the skills of detailed analysis, case study production, innovation, creativity, clarity of thought, and high-quality presentation that good researchers develop early on in their careers.

From a managerial perspective, academics need time and space to be good teachers. In other words, they need time to develop their teaching materials and lectures and they need offices with sufficient peace and quiet to think and create. Universities that pack academics into large, noisy open-plan offices and insist that they teach in front of a class for 15-plus hours a week will not have high-quality teaching.

As a department head or dean, you need to be wary of trying to "sweat the assets" too much. It can backfire in an overall reduction in teaching quality and student satisfaction, which can result in lower enrolments, reduced budgets, and the tendency to sweat the assets even harder. This can be a vicious circle of decline for any university department.

Setting Academic Workloads

One of the most difficult challenges for heads of academic departments is assigning duties to individual academics and ensuring that they all have a broadly equivalent workload. While academics are largely self-directed in regard to their research and how they teach (which is a good thing), what they teach will be dictated by the curriculum of a particular degree programme. There will be expectations of a certain number of hours of formal teaching, as well as time devoted to informal student contact and academic administration.

Heads of department have the unenviable duty each semester of trying to determine what duties should be assigned to each member of staff, taking into account their expertise, seniority, suitability for certain administrative responsibilities, how much research they do, and whether or not they have external obligations such as funded research or consultancy projects to undertake.

Many institutions try to use models that allocate hours per week for specific work activities and try to ensure that the total number of hours worked by each academic are broadly equivalent. In practice, such models rarely work well and arguments about who does what and how many hours they should be allocated for each duty are commonplace.

I have always taken the view that to defuse arguments over academic workloads, it is best if a model is developed at departmental rather than institutional level and that the model is "owned" by the entire academic staff team of the department. It should not be devised and controlled solely by the head. It should be a model that the staff collectively buy into as a fair way of dividing activities between themselves, overseen by the head.

It is best if workloads are transparent and shared openly so that everyone can see in broad terms what everyone else is doing. If one person has half the number of teaching hours of someone else in a given week, the reason for that should be entirely clear to everyone. There is no perfect workload model even though many institutions, in my experience, try to find one. It is a bit like the never-ending search for the holy grail.

In my view, the responsibility of the institution as a whole is to ensure that each department is resourced fairly in terms of its academic staff number. A centralised resourcing model should be used to determine this based on income generated, student numbers, research grants won, etc. Once the staffing number has been fixed for a department, however, it is down to the individuals in that department—facilitated by their head—to figure out how to divide workloads among themselves in a way that is as fair as possible, recognising that the complexity and multiplicity of activities in a typical academic department rarely enables 100% fairness to be achieved.

CHAPTER 4

Managing Students as Business Partners

The University Customer Experience

Increasingly, as universities in many countries are required to charge higher and higher fees for their degrees, students and their parents or guardians see themselves as "customers" of the university. This shift towards students viewing themselves as customers or even consumers of education means that they expect a high-quality experience for their money as well as a high-quality outcome in terms of a good degree.

Students, and often their parents as well, not only expect a good experience and outcome but also demand it and can become very dissatisfied, and indeed on occasions belligerent, if they do not get it. As an academic manager, you therefore have to adopt a mindset of delivering a service to demanding customers who expect to be satisfied. This may not necessarily be how you viewed education when you were a student, but times have changed. Whether this change is for the better I leave to you to decide.

In most fields of business or commerce, customers buy a service or product and expect it to be of good quality and fit for purpose. However, in higher education, the customers are buying the right to be taught and supported but the ultimate product, that is the academic qualification, depends on their own hard work and ability. This is a sophisticated and prolonged engagement, not simply buying something and walking away. This makes higher education fundamentally different to most other commercial activities in regard to its relationship with its customers.

To put this in perspective, imagine what the relationship between a customer and a car dealer might be if, on ordering a luxury car, the company simply provided the tools, materials, and training but asked the customer to go to a manufacturing plant and assemble it himself or herself. This is effectively what happens in higher education: the university and the student jointly create the product, that is the award of a degree. That product may also be relatively expensive, on a par with purchasing a luxury car in some cases. Students are thus business partners, co-producing the end result.

This is quite unlike most commercial activities and puts the university in a difficult situation. Effectively, to create a strong sense of customer satisfaction, a university must use all means available to encourage students to work effectively as partners in delivering the final, expensive product: the degree. If the final product is not what was expected, the student may be tempted to blame the university for failing to deliver the desired outcome even if in reality it is the student's own fault for failing to study hard enough. Operating in such a challenging environment can present significant problems for the university's managers. Essentially, these problems centre on creating a shared sense of responsibility with the customers—the students— and managing their expectations.

In exploring the university-customer relationship, it is necessary to focus on two aspects of the engagement, namely the overall quality of the day-to-day service experienced and the quality of the final product received. With regard to the former, the responsibility for quality lies primarily with the university; with the latter, the responsibility is largely shared.

> **A university must use all means available to encourage students to work effectively as partners in delivering the final, expensive product: the degree.**

In managing students not merely as customers but as business partners, it is extremely important for you to understand what students are experiencing and ensuring that everything is done to optimise the experience. Good managers in higher education are able to imagine themselves in the shoes of the students and understand what the students see and feel on a day-to-day basis. They listen to the "student voice". They can then relate well to the students and understand any difficulties they may be experiencing, which comes back to the use of EI. It is also possible to learn a lot from student surveys and through studying student sentiment on social media.

Good institutions will survey all of their students about their general experiences on a regular basis, such as every semester or at least annually. Such surveys ideally cover all aspects of university life including teaching and learning, study support, infrastructure, library and other learning resources, social and sporting facilities, accommodation, induction procedures, campus information technology (IT) facilities, and career support. They will also survey students on individual courses about their specific learning experiences.

If you want to be a really good manager in higher education, you should value the feedback you receive from students and take action to deal with any problems or unhappiness that is revealed. Once action has been taken it is then good practice to ensure that students understand what has been fixed and how. Feedback on remedies to issues helps instil confidence in the student body. Students also need to believe that their views are taken seriously, that they are true partners in the education process, and that positive changes can come from constructive criticism.

If the feedback loop is broken and if either issues are not fixed or information on remedies is not given, student opinion will be negative, which can be institutionally damaging and reflect badly on the particular department or faculty with the problem and ultimately also on the relevant academic manager. All of this should be fairly obvious to most good academic managers, but experience reveals that it often is not.

Regrettably, some managers in higher education still take the mistaken and outdated view that students are there to learn from the experts and that the quality of service is relatively unimportant. There can be an expressed arrogance along the lines of "these students are very lucky to be here and to have the benefit of my wisdom—if they fail that is their problem, not mine".

Even if managers do not take such a view, some of the staff that they manage may do so and this can require managerial action to rectify such an attitude. In the era of social media, staff who come over as arrogant or disrespectful to students in any way will soon be broadcast to the world and students will literally avoid their classes or even the university. It does not take many negative or badly behaved staff to do significant damage to a university.

Part of the problem is that as universities focus increasingly on their global rankings and need academics to deliver more in terms of research, the quality of the service to the students can go down. If academic managers press too hard on achieving research output and grant income, academic staff may feel forced into reducing the time they make available for students, or perhaps into cutting corners in their preparation of teaching materials.

The tension between teaching and research that pulls academics in different directions is a significant challenge in many institutions and one that university managers have to struggle with on a constant basis. The organisational challenge of delivering both high-quality research and high-quality customer service to students in regard to teaching is an enormous one.

At the level of an academic department, a head will need to work with the academic staff to come up with a locally workable solution. This might involve asking some staff to focus mainly on research and others mainly on teaching and student support. Alternatively, it might be determined that everyone should contribute in all areas and has to work out how to divide their time. As discussed in Chapter 3, managers such as department heads and deans need to develop and agree fair workload models that all their staff can buy into, which is often easier said than done. Ideally, as a manager, this is something you would do collectively through a collaborative process.

Managing Diversity

One aspect of managing students that has become very important in recent years is managing diversity, which is becoming more significant as a result of globalisation. As higher education has expanded and become more international, institutions are bringing in more and more students from highly diverse backgrounds. This may be in terms of ethnicity, religion, sexual orientation, social class, income, physical disability, and geographical origin. The spectrum is very wide and institutions must adapt how they work to welcome all comers.

Managers have to be particularly sensitive to cultural issues and ensure that neither they themselves, nor their staff, unwittingly reveal prejudices, biases, or lack of cultural understanding. Great care has to be taken to ensure that all students get fair and equal access to opportunities on campus and are not, in any way, made to feel inferior or lose dignity. This is something that you need to be totally committed to as a manager. You need to ensure that you create and maintain a completely unbiased educational environment in all aspects so that everyone feels comfortable and is able to fully engage in the educational process.

Caring for Students' Mental Health

Another important aspect of managing students involves taking care of their mental well-being. Universities are large communities and there will always be a small number of students facing mental health problems. It is essential to look out for such cases and refer them to appropriate channels if necessary, such as counselling and health services. Ensuring that students with mental health issues receive appropriate support and guidance is essential to prevent their situation deteriorating.

Sadly, occurrences of suicides are rising globally among young people and universities occasionally have to deal with such cases. Most institutions have counselling services available to support students with mental health problems. Often such problems arise from relationship issues or external pressures compounding the stresses of a challenging degree course. It is important to recognise that for many students, their time at university is their first real opportunity to break from parental control and the first time they become relatively independent. This can be, and often is, a time of stress as they adapt to their new situation in life.

The More Challenging Customers

Inevitably, managers in higher education will from time to time encounter challenging students and parents; the latter sometimes testing institutional customer-handling procedures to the extreme. Students can be demanding and sometimes appear unreasonably so and this is an attribute sometimes associated by older academics with millennials, though there is little justification for this.

In dealing with unreasonable demands it is always essential to fall back to rules and regulations, and to follow due process in any complaints. If necessary, a manager should be prepared to take a pragmatic decision, based on the principles of fairness and justice, to ensure that a student receives the kind of treatment that any third-party, fair-minded person would expect. Sometimes this can mean going outside of rules or regulations if they appear too rigid and not sufficiently flexible to deal with any unusual situations that occur, as we shall discuss later in relation to complex decision-making.

Parents can be challenging for university managers as they sometimes take an excessively intrusive interest in their child's education and development. University students are effectively independent adults in law and should be treated as such by universities. However, this does not stop many parents from probing the university about their son's or daughter's progress and potentially interfering in making complaints or appeals about assessment grades, etc. Parents can be very demanding if they feel that their child is not getting the support and care that they expect. When a son's or daughter's future career prospects are at stake, parents can become extremely vociferous and challenging to deal with.

University managers need to deal with such parents diplomatically, treading the difficult line between being supportive to the parents but not unreasonably revealing confidential information about a student or the student's progress that the student would not want revealed. This may need some delicate handling.

It is advisable always for you to get a sense from the student how much parental interaction he or she is willing to tolerate before engaging in too much dialogue or information sharing with a parent. Some parents who demand access to information beyond the level the student is prepared to share need to be dealt with sensitively but firmly if necessary.

Universities normally reserve the right to restrict their interactions to students if it becomes so necessary, on the basis that they are independent adults, and not engage directly with parents or guardians. The situation is complex because parents are often the ones paying for the student's education, but data protection laws may limit what they can be told. As a manager, you may have to tread a delicate path of trying to stay within the law, deal with parental concerns, and keep students happy all at the same time. There may be conflicting agendas at play. Tact, diplomacy, and using EI (as always) are paramount.

CHAPTER 5

Finding and Keeping the Stellar Cats

Recruiting the Right Staff

The recruitment of academic staff is arguably one of the most important duties of managers in higher education. Institutional success is primarily determined by the quality and capability of staff, not by budgets, infrastructure, or anything else—although such factors are not unrelated in that a strong budget and high-quality infrastructure help to attract good staff. So, if you want an easy life as an academic manager, get the right staff and you would have won half the battle. Time spent in recruiting the right people is time saved later many times over in terms of managing the institution.

Fundamentally, good academic staff teach well, research well, interact with students well, and present the institution in a good light to the outside world. It is of high priority always to seek the best academic staff that you can whenever vacancies occur. In practice, it pays to spend time and money on searching for good staff, as opposed to making a quick appointment of a less-than-ideal candidate. Once appointed, academic staff may be in post for as long as 40 years if recruited in their twenties. It is clearly better to take months over recruitment to seek out the right person than to make a bad appointment that lasts decades.

Finding the right academic staff is always a challenge for an academic manager. It is a case of finding academics who have the right subject knowledge at the forefront of their disciplines, as well as the right personality to fit in with colleagues and students and help move the institution forward in regard to its key agendas, such as improving teaching quality, growing its research base, or developing its industrial links. Recruitment needs to operate effectively and transparently, and should normally involve a global search if you want to get the best.

Finding people with in-depth knowledge really necessitates a global search because the number of highly qualified individuals in any one individual country will be limited. Even where a good number of such individuals exist in a country, the proportion who are prepared to be mobile and move to a new institution may be rather small. Looking globally for the most talented academics is therefore obligatory if an institution is ambitious and aiming for high quality in its teaching and research.

Whenever a recruitment campaign is conducted, the recruiting manager needs to write an accurate and precise job description as well as advertisements and documents describing the institutional context and what is expected from the recruit. These documents need to be written in such a way as to appeal to highly talented individuals in the international context. It is no good writing an advertisement that only makes sense to individuals in your own country if the idea is to conduct a global recruitment campaign.

Looking globally for the most talented academics is therefore obligatory if an institution is ambitious.

Managing applicants well is another key aspect of recruiting high-quality staff. Often many tens, if not hundreds, of applicants will apply for good academic jobs. It is always essential to conduct shortlisting fairly against objective criteria and to ensure that any rejected applicants are treated reasonably. This means providing objective and realistic feedback if requested. Badly treated applicants can become your worst enemies and ultimately might even use their negativity to influence outcomes for your institution such as negatively reviewing grant applications or research papers.

Handling interviews is a sensitive process. It is wise to interview enough candidates to have some element of choice, and to compare candidates who appear to have similar strengths, at least on paper. However, it is unwise to interview too many candidates as this can waste their time as well as yours. Getting it right is a difficult balancing act. It is also inadvisable to bring in too many candidates from overseas as that can indeed waste enormous amounts of time for the individuals concerned, as well as incur significant costs in terms of flights and hotel rooms.

If you have many strong candidates from overseas it is wise to conduct short interviews of a long list via Skype, or similar internet-based video conferencing system, and only bring a selected few to campus for a physical interview. In my experience, unsuccessful candidates flown long haul internationally for interviews can become extremely irate if turned down. They always need to be treated with respect and gratitude to deflect significant potential negative sentiment.

Successful candidates also need to be treated well to help them adjust to their new academic home. Straight after the interview process, they need to be given clear offers specifying the precise benefits and expectations of the role and also be given every opportunity to learn about the institution to ensure that they can be confident they are making the right move. They also need effective induction and mentoring in the early months to help them settle in their new working environment.

Handling all aspects of recruitment and onboarding well is truly an important aspect of being a good manager in higher education. It sometimes takes the experience of a few recruitment cycles to do it well, but learning from the process will bring dividends in terms of building high-performing teams and taking a department, faculty, or even whole institution forward effectively.

Managing the Most Senior "Star" Academics

Although it is often not fully recognised, universities are essentially defined in terms of global standing by the quality and knowledge of their most senior academics. Without their distinguished academic staff, the most revered academic institutions, such as the Ivy League institutions in the United States (USA) or Oxbridge in the UK, would be no more than community colleges. Their ancient classical style buildings would mean nothing. The higher the quality of the academic staff overall, the higher the quality, reputation, and international ranking of the institution.

> **Universities are essentially defined in terms of global standing by the quality and knowledge of their most senior academics.**

Just as football teams are defined by their star players and movies are largely defined by the stars in the cast, universities are to a large extent defined by their star academics. The top-ranking global universities compete to attract the academic superstars, such as the Nobel Prize winners, the Fields Medal winners, the authors of seminal academic texts, and the theorists whose ideas have changed the world.

Even lesser universities need to compete to attract good quality academics whose experience and academic standing will help the university grow in status. Academics with significant reputations, even a long way from the level of the Nobel Laureate, can still bring huge benefits to universities. They are more likely, on average, to be able to attract research funding. They will have more interesting ideas to present to the media. They will be able to attract younger aspiring academics to join their departments or research groups.

Managing the academic "stars" is thus a key element of managing universities. Good universities must attract academic stars, even superstars, retain them, nurture them, and allow them to grow. They are the bedrock on which a successful university can develop.

Recruiting the most senior academic staff to a university is one of the most important activities to be managed well. Heads of department and deans need to recognise that getting the right senior academics may well define their success or failure over a period of a number of years. It is often said that success breeds success and that is especially true in academia. Already successful and accomplished academics can bring their reputation and success to a new institution willing to recruit them.

Recruitment of the most senior academics, for example at the level of full professor, needs to be managed extremely well. Sometimes these individuals will be expected to fulfil a management role such as leading a research group, department, or faculty. Whatever role is expected of them, the managers in charge of recruiting must do their utmost to attract the most talented individuals to join. The management of the recruitment process is a key aspect of this.

In some cases, it may be appropriate to use headhunting agencies. Though, in my experience, this can give mixed results. Headhunters are not always good at identifying the best academic talent as few actually understand highly talented academics and will subject them to personality tests which headhunters have been told work well in selecting senior executives in other industries and so ought to work in academia.

> **Good universities must attract academic stars, even superstars, retain them, nurture them and allow them to grow.**

It is particularly important to conduct a global search when looking for academic stars. Outstanding academics usually consider themselves globally mobile and open to offers from anywhere if the terms and benefits are right. Of course, many will be rather fussy about what kind of institution they are prepared to join looking for top brands, but others will be more open to joining lesser-known institutions if the compensation is attractive enough.

There is little point in looking for the most senior academics in one country alone. It is now extremely easy to advertise globally through some of the excellent online academic recruitment websites. Apart from advertising, institutions can do their own headhunting by seeking out individuals from their web profiles, if the particular requirements of the post are defined clearly.

One of the most challenging aspects of recruiting academic stars is the level and type of compensation. Just as in football or Hollywood, the higher the quality and reputation of the star, the higher the price is likely to be to attract them. It has to be appreciated by managers in universities that if they wish to recruit top talent, they will have to offer appropriate remuneration that may well be outside of normal levels. Stars may need astronomical benefits.

A manager such as a department head or faculty dean needs to take a difficult decision over what kind of compensation package to offer. Sometimes it may be necessary to pay well above the level of other staff in the department or faculty, and sometimes even well above the level of equivalently ranked staff in the whole university. A balanced decision has to be taken in which the benefits of taking on the preferred candidate are weighed against the cost.

Sometimes as a head or dean, you may find it necessary to pay a new professor more than you yourself are paid. Although this can be a bitter pill to swallow, good managers recognise that their job is to maximise the opportunities for their departments or faculties and, if that means bringing in someone paid higher than themselves, this is not a problem even if it can be uncomfortable. It is just a consequence of seeking out academic stars and recruiting them to take the institution forward. Furthermore, if the department or faculty grows overall in reputation as a result of the higher-paid academic stars, everyone (and not just the stars) can potentially gain from the enhanced reputation, increasing everyone's future career prospects.

Sometimes stars can be attracted by factors other than pure remuneration, for example, special titles such as "distinguished professor". Also, academics can be attracted by the offer of dedicated facilities, such as laboratories, or even the offer of funded fellowships for a team of researchers to work with them. Such means can be used to attract the stars that the institution feels will bring significant benefits.

Attracting the most senior academics is only part of the challenge for university managers. Retaining them can be even more of a challenge. There are several dimensions to this. Firstly, academic stars are well aware that they have international value and are generally not afraid of being dismissed.

Secondly, they also consider themselves to be outstanding in their fields and expect immeasurable respect for it, sometimes verging almost on worship. They certainly do not like to feel they are objects to be managed and indeed are likely to be resistant to any form of management that looks like control. There is, in essence, a kind of uneasy pact between a university and its best academic stars—both parties need each other, but also each has to tolerate the needs of the other.

For example, the department or faculty may need the star to teach certain classes. The star, on the other hand, needs considerable flexibility to undertake his or her own activities, especially research, without interference and with a sufficient level of resources. If all goes well and each can be sufficiently tolerant of the other, then the university will gain considerably.

It may be particularly challenging, however, for a younger or less experienced manager to cope with this situation well, particularly if the academic star shows little respect for his or her manager. Such situations can put less experienced managers under a lot of stress, but they need to stand back from the situation and recognise that making it work, even if he or she has to swallow his or her pride on many occasions, is in the greater interest of the university as a whole.

Apart from respect and flexibility, academic stars will normally expect to be given the freedom to undertake activities outside of the university. This can range from participating in national (or even international) committees or advisory groups to undertaking consultancy. The latter can be a particularly thorny issue as some less enlightened universities expect their staff to work exclusively for the university.

Academic stars, however, are unlikely to accept that at face value. They recognise that their knowledge is in demand and will expect to be allowed to share it or apply it through consultancy work for external clients. This helps them as individuals to assert their pre-eminence in their fields and become better known. If consultancy is offered, they like to feel that they are the ones selected by the client to undertake it because they are really good at what they do. It is as much a confidence boost as an opportunity to share their knowledge, but the university may not always see it that way.

An enlightened university will recognise that having its academics, especially its most expert ones, undertake consultancy is an important mechanism to boost their reputations. By undertaking work for external clients, they become more widely known and respected from which the university will gain indirectly.

The issue of payment for such activities can be an area of contention. If a university permits its academics to undertake consultancy but then demands all or most of the payment for the work that has been undertaken, then the consultancy will essentially be driven underground. The academic stars will still do it but as a private arrangement between themselves and their clients. This situation is very commonly found and in such a situation the academic gains personally but the university loses everything.

It is far better for outstanding academics to be allowed to undertake paid consultancy using the university's name and time with the financial reward shared. If managed well, the university can gain through being seen to offer the consultancy services of its expert staff. In doing this, the university should only expect to take a small slice of the income generated, allowing the lion's share to go to the academic. After all, the academic is the one whose reputation gave rise to the consultancy in the first place and whose initiative in following up a lead has led to the work being undertaken.

Good universities and good managers recognise this and allow their best academics to undertake consultancy and retain most of the earnings from it. The academics enjoy the recognition coming from the client organisation as well as the opportunity to boost their income. The university gains from links generated with the client and, through word of mouth, acquires a reputation as an institution that is supportive of external companies. These intangible benefits make it highly worthwhile, allowing academics to undertake consultancy in the name of the university and on very generous terms to the academics involved.

CHAPTER 6

Managing Entrepreneurially

The Need for Universities to Be Entrepreneurial

All good managers in universities should be aware of the need to contribute to the development of the entire organisation and not only a small part of it. Good universities do not stand still and normally seek to grow in size, status, or reputation. They will also often have to adapt to changing circumstances such as changes in their external regulatory environment, changes to funding regimes, or shifting demand patterns for courses, among many others. This requires you to manage entrepreneurially and to lead change effectively.

The concept of being entrepreneurial is not something that may naturally be associated with universities. Indeed, many academics may not think of themselves as entrepreneurs. Yet being entrepreneurial is essential for most universities to prosper and the most successful organisations in the world tend to be those that have a deeply embedded entrepreneurial culture.

Entrepreneurial organisations have a strong focus on their products or services. They ensure that they have a constant stream of new products or services that are better than anything offered by their competitors, and ideally better value for money as well. That is the key to staying in business or getting ahead of competitors.

The failure to remain entrepreneurial has been the root cause of the demise of many well-known companies. In *The New Entrepreneurial Age*,[14] Larry C. Farrell says organisations go through four phases in their life cycle: start-up, high growth, decline, and survival. Companies that fail to stay entrepreneurial will soon progress to the decline phase and eventually struggle to survive.

Farrell makes a further very important point that as organisations grow, they become increasingly managerial and bureaucratic. This in itself can stifle innovation and the entrepreneurial culture. University managers need to be aware of this. Building successful universities means ensuring they maintain a strong entrepreneurial culture long-term and not be overly bureaucratic.

This analysis is relevant to many universities though arguably not all. Universities that are perceived to be world-class, for example, those in the top 0.1% globally, are likely to continue to attract students, come what may. Their brands are so strong that their customers will come no matter what "products" they have to offer. Anecdotally, some bright students apply to study degrees at certain elite universities in subjects that are relatively unpopular and often irrelevant to their desired careers, such as theology or classical languages, just to be sure of gaining entry. The university *brand* is far more important to them than the product (i.e., the degree). The institution's name is a badge of honour or form of status signalling that stays with the graduate forever regardless of what was studied.

This privileged status, however, does not apply to the vast majority of universities in the world. Most need to work hard to attract students in order to keep operating successfully and that means, fundamentally, being entrepreneurial or "intrapreneurial" in the sense of being entrepreneurial within a large organisation. This applies equally to public- and private-sector universities.

No public university will continue for long unquestioned if it loses its students. Ultimately a government body will intervene and replace the senior management or force a merger or even closure, though the latter is extremely rare. Likewise, no private university can continue in business if it starts to haemorrhage students. The governors or directors will be forced to act in order to protect the interests of shareholders, foundations, or other funding bodies. In any but the most distinguished global brand-name universities, it is relatively easy for a spiral of decline to occur if a university does not behave entrepreneurially.

Students will normally seek out the most interesting and relevant degrees for their future careers. Degrees that are perceived as old-fashioned, boring, or unrelated to contemporary job opportunities will soon lose market share. Any academic university manager needs to be well aware of this. The decline in interest in a department's or faculty's programmes can soon lead to closure. As student numbers fall, there are fewer graduates to tell other potential applicants about the course and soon there is a downward spiral.

A decline can affect individual departments, faculties, or entire universities. Normally it will start with individual departments, but if this decline in one academic area is symptomatic of a tired un-enterprising culture across the whole institution then serious consequences can arise.

The need to avoid decline and to be entrepreneurial is something that, as a manager in a 21st-century university, you need to embrace. Bad news about universities and their programmes spreads easily through social media. Also, students are much more mobile than they used to be and are increasingly willing and able to travel considerable distances to gain the specific education they desire. Hence, universities can no longer take it for granted that the young people within their natural hinterland will continue to turn up at their doors.

The state of being entrepreneurial requires staff at all levels and in all functions to think and act entrepreneurially at all times. This means being alert to what competing institutions are doing, being creative in designing new academic programmes with a strong market appeal, and looking at new ways of academic delivery.[15] A truly entrepreneurial university will be doing these all the time. It will also focus on developing strong links with industry to generate revenue from consulting, applied research, training, and other forms of knowledge transfer. Some institutions have become highly successful in this[16] and take pride in developing their stakeholder base as a means of institutional growth.

The role of an academic manager is to ensure that staff in his or her department or faculty are aware of the need to behave entrepreneurially, and to recognise and reward those that are. Such behaviour will enable the institution to continue its mission, stay in business if private, and even grow. Cultivating entrepreneurial behaviour in relation to courses may not always be easy as some academics are happy to continue teaching what they have taught many times before and may not perceive the need for change. They may not want to develop new programmes or teach new material because it requires extra time and effort they would rather devote to something else such as research.

> **The state of being entrepreneurial requires staff at all levels and in all functions to think and act entrepreneurially at all times.**

You have to be sensitive to the feelings of academics in this regard, but still be able to put over tactfully the message that without innovation in courses, the department or faculty will face serious financial problems and that ultimately their jobs may be at risk. Staff often do not connect students with their salaries, but they should.

It is often the case that academics, in particular, get used to a relatively cosy environment in which their jobs seem to go on forever no matter what happens. The nature of academic tenure, which effectively gives permanent employment rights, has encouraged such feelings. However, even where academic tenure exists (an increasingly rare situation), tenure can be broken if a department or institution is under threat. No permanent contract of employment is worth much if a department has to close. The job of an academic manager is not to scaremonger, but to ensure that everyone knows the necessity of innovation and being entrepreneurial.

The role of senior management is to ensure overall that staff at all levels, and in all roles, understand that they need to be entrepreneurial. This applies equally to operational service managers as to academic managers. It is of no use at all having entrepreneurial academics if the service departments do not respond and work with them

> **The role of senior management is to ensure that staff at all levels, and in all roles, understand that they need to be entrepreneurial.**

to ensure that new products (i.e., new degrees) are introduced in a timely fashion. This means supporting new programmes through internal and external approval procedures (when required), ensuring appropriate resources are put in place (e.g., library books, IT systems, laboratory resources), and ensuring that new programmes are effectively marketed.

Change Management

Inevitably, universities will undergo periods of intense change, whether they are behaving entrepreneurially or not. Most universities are deeply conservative institutions and are not places where change usually occurs rapidly. In some cases, they have structures, roles, procedures, and processes that were established many decades or even centuries ago and have changed little since.

Academics are comfortable with traditions and stability and, if there is change, they expect to agree to it through wide or unanimous consensus. A stable environment enables academics to focus on what they really enjoy doing most, which is teaching and researching. Often the ways of doing things have become embedded through custom and practice over many years.

Even in the more recently established institutions, many procedures and operating formalities may have been modelled on longer-established universities. Whether or not the procedures have been borrowed or newly created, it is still unlikely that they will change much from year to year. The clever people who inhabit universities want to keep the house stable so they can thrive doing academic things.

Ambitious newly appointed managers in universities can sometimes find themselves in a challenging environment. Often, they are keen to make a mark and want to change something that they perceive as ineffective or inefficient. They may be eager to move the institution forward and ensure that their area of responsibility is seen as moving with the times.

The eagerness to implement change can then become a source of disquiet among staff members, especially long-serving ones. First and foremost the job of a manager is to ensure stability and a harmonious working environment, while also facilitating innovation and entrepreneurial behaviour. A good manager achieves both. While change is often highly desirable or even necessary to move the department, faculty, or university forward, it has to be done at a pace that does not lead to significant unrest.

Universities are places where staff and students can be very vocal in opposing change and are capable of putting up highly intelligent and well-thought-out arguments as to why a proposed change will not work. New managers, therefore,

> **First and foremost, the job of a manager is to ensure stability and a harmonious working environment.**

need to be on their guard and not push change too fast. Even changes that seem entirely logical and obvious can lead to unease with some very powerful counterarguments being put up against their implementation.

New university managers should, in the first instance, spend a substantial amount of time learning about their institution, how it works, where it is going, and what its strategic objectives are. They need to understand in detail what is going on in their particular area of management responsibility as well as operating procedures—who does what, who controls what. They also need to understand any policies, regulations, or procedures that apply, when these were first implemented, and who was responsible for developing them. Being highly complex organisations, it is quite possible that policies or procedures that a new manager may wish to introduce already exist, but that he or she has simply not found them yet.

Only after very detailed knowledge has been acquired should a new manager start to implement change. The first few months of a new manager's job will thus be one of observing, gathering information, and learning. In the vast majority of cases, a new manager should not dive into the deep end, trying to tackle big issues straightaway.

The best approach is to learn about the current situation and slowly come to some conclusions about what changes might be needed. Normally this requires initial informal discussions with members of the manager's team, but may ultimately require more extensive consultation. Sometimes this consultation will be done with ad hoc staff team meetings, other times formal discussions and decisions at committees.

It cannot be emphasised strongly enough how necessary the key steps of observing, learning, discussing, and consulting are before any changes are put forward for implementation. This is so important in the university context because of the intelligence of the body of workers and students and of their capability to question, debate, and challenge. Without taking the time, departmental or institutional stability can be put at risk. It is relatively easy for a new manager to cause a significant industrial relations problem and a breakdown of trust between staff and management.

For example, a new manager who senses that a particular member of staff is not pulling his or her weight and then rashly threatens him or her with contract

> **Observing, learning, discussing, and consulting are necessary before implementing changes.**

termination may think the behavioural problem will soon be solved. Instead, this naïve and inexperienced manager is likely to find himself or herself subject to a collective grievance raised by a group of staff or their union or staff association. This can drag the manager's superiors into solving an industrial relations crisis which is not something they want to be spending their time doing. Ultimately the manager who caused the problem is likely to have to back down and will lose face with the staff team in the process as well as a certain amount of credibility with his or her own manager.

Getting the pace right on a change is an important issue for any new manager to address. Sensitivity to the institutional context is paramount. Does he or she want to change something that has been embedded for centuries or something that was introduced two years ago? This may give some guidance as to how fast to make a change. Regardless of the pace of change, gaining the support of key constituencies within departments and faculties is a key element in introducing a change effectively and for this, a manager needs time to develop alliances.

Another key factor in controlling the pace of change is how important the change is to the core mission of the university. Will the students or the institution's reputation suffer immediately if the change is not made right now? Managers should not rush into changing practices or procedures that have served the institution well for a long time. Neither should they rush to change things that actually do not make a lot of difference to the core mission of the institution.

Good managers are contemplative, measured, and circumspect in making changes and always consult key stakeholders carefully. Managers who can do this will undoubtedly have successful careers and climb the managerial hierarchy. Universities seeking new academic managers will always be on the lookout for candidates who implemented change carefully in their previous institutions and successfully helped the university evolve while maintaining peace and stability along the way. Rash managers who cause problems and instability end up being sidelined in their careers, particularly if they do not learn from early mistakes.

One of the key elements to leading change in a university is to do it with passion and charisma. It is undoubtedly true that many managers who make it to the upper echelons in universities have considerable charisma and show a real passion for what they do. These qualities have enabled them to shine in front of selection panels and achieve their (normally) richly deserved promotions.

Charismatic managers, especially at the most senior levels, can often inspire their staff greatly and garner support from a wide range of external stakeholders for institutional developments. In most cases, they are huge assets to their institutions. They are also often very good with the media and can generate a lot of interest in the work of the university from far and wide.

Sometimes, however, the possession of charisma and the ability to show (or perhaps feign) passion can lead to otherwise inadequate managers being promoted to levels where their charisma exceeds their competence by a very wide margin. This can lead to serious managerial problems for others to deal with.

Charismatic, highly confident, but incompetent managers are few and far between in universities, yet they do exist and can be a major challenge for those around them, especially if they have been fortunate or lucky enough to reach the most senior level of management. Situations in which such senior managers have to be removed do occur. Votes of "no confidence" in a senior manager by the staff are not uncommon in universities, even in some of the most distinguished universities in the world.

Readers who do not consider themselves charismatic should not fear that their futures are blighted because of it. In fact, many highly successful university managers are relatively quiet, introspective individuals. Success in the university context, at least for academics in the early phase of their careers, often relies on success in research. The best researchers are often the staff who put in the effort in the laboratory or the library, working away diligently for long hours almost in solitude. Also, for those with teaching-focused careers, labouring in isolation preparing inspirational teaching materials can lead to recognition and promotion.

Such individuals can indeed become very high achievers. They are able to do the detailed work behind the scenes and, in the right setting, able to convey their thoughts or findings in a most convincing way to audiences. There are numerous examples of highly successful and distinguished academics with retiring or shy personalities who could, in the right setting, enthral an audience.

There is little doubt that it is not necessary for a high-quality university manager to be extroverted, charismatic, or flamboyant in character though it can be helpful.

Simplistic views of what might make a good senior manager in the corporate world do not always extrapolate into the university context.

Selection panels for senior managers need to be wary of relying on superficial evidence of managerial ability. Research has shown that humans can substantially overestimate the future likely performance of individuals from very limited evidence. This effect, known as the "Illusion of Valid Prediction", is well documented by the Nobel Laureate Daniel Kahneman in his compelling book *Thinking, Fast and Slow*.[17] In my opinion, this should be compulsory reading for search committees for senior management roles in universities.

CHAPTER 7
Managing Finances

The Importance of Finance

Even though many academics and administrators in universities may not like to admit it, the undeniable truth is that money really does "make the world go around", to quote from a song from the 1972 musical drama film *Cabaret*. The management of financial resources is a fundamental part of the job of any university manager; no money equals no university!

Almost all managers in universities will have some responsibility for managing a budget, and most will have the additional responsibility of helping to generate income for the organisation by encouraging their teams to produce bids for research grants or industrial projects. In some countries, many managers at senior levels will be expected to support the generation of income from philanthropic sources and to spend some of their time cultivating relationships with wealthy potential donors and alumni, as well as in developing proposals that such donors might wish to support.

No one can be blind to the fact that any university is resource-constrained and has to live within its means. Some universities are clearly much better off than others with substantial endowments, investments, and cash reserves, in some cases built up over centuries. Others may operate on a knife-edge with very little in reserve and with a very fine balance between annual income and expenditure. Regardless of whether any particular university is financially well-positioned or not, every manager within it must take financial resource management very seriously. There are a number of aspects to financial resource management that we shall consider in turn.

Understanding the basic financial regime in which the institution is operating is the first requirement. Is it a state institution relying primarily on public funds? Or alternatively, is it a private institution? If the latter, does it have to make a profit for its shareholders? Or is it perhaps owned by a non-profit-making charitable foundation? These are key questions and any responsible manager in a university needs to know which regime applies.

Besides comprehending the basic financial framework, it is extremely important to understand the current financial status of the institution and whether or not it is meeting its financial objectives. To understand this, it is vital to know what the main sources of income are, whether they are growing or decreasing, and whether the institution is actually making a surplus/profit or deficit/ loss. The financial status is important in assessing the risk level posed by the institution to its main stakeholders and how much pressure it is likely to come under from those stakeholders if the financial status is deteriorating.

Understanding Institutional Macro-Finance

Sources of income for universities will typically fall into several categories: government grants for teaching and research; student fees; income from business services such as consultancy or training; returns generated by investments, royalties, or licensing fees from intellectual property (IP) exploitation; income from miscellaneous services such as hostel or property rental and food and beverage services on campus; and finally income from philanthropy (i.e., charitable donations) typically from alumni.

No two universities are exactly alike in the division of income between these categories. Apart from the division between categories, the absolute magnitude of the sums involved will differ enormously from one institution to another. Some universities have gross turnover figures of the order of billions of dollars; others of only a few tens of millions of dollars. The financial scales can be very different.

Apart from understanding the sources of income, as a manager, you ought to know whether the sums coming from the various sources are secure, whether they are growing or decreasing, and what the financial future of the university looks like. Is the university able to cover its current costs and its likely future costs? Will it generate a sufficient profit for its shareholders (if it has any)? Will it generate sufficient surplus to invest in new facilities and developments, of whatever kind? Also, how would these affect you and the part of the institution that you lead?

These are key questions about the macro-financial position of the university that any manager needs to understand because they impact on the day-to-day micro-financial decisions that any manager must take. These questions also impact on the likelihood that the manager will be able to invest in some new development project, such as starting a new degree programme, or add some new resource, such as a new piece of capital equipment for a laboratory.

Income volatility needs to be understood at all levels of the university. Some of the sources of income can fluctuate wildly in relation to the vagaries of the market for the institution's services. For example, foreign student fee income can fluctuate significantly following currency movements or changes in national immigration control, aspects which are largely outside of the control of the university.

A good understanding of the macro-financial position is essential for the effective taking of micro-financial decisions. A good manager never forgets the macro-financial position of the institution and his or her role in protecting or improving that position. Surprisingly, many managers in contemporary universities behave as though the overall financial position is of no concern of theirs. Nothing could be further from the truth. Every university manager who ignores the overall financial position of the institution does a great disservice to his or her colleagues as he or she is likely to make rash decisions which increase the financial instability of the institution.

> **A good manager never forgets the macro-financial position of the institution and his or her role in protecting or improving that position.**

Quite simply, a good university manager has a good grasp of the finances as they apply to the university overall and to his or her own area of responsibility, but the number of managers who have this is limited from my experience. Those who do can expect considerable respect from their superiors and are likely to find their future career prospects as managers and leaders enhanced.

To be a good manager, it is essential to pay attention to the financial viability of your unit or area of responsibility. You will normally oversee discipline areas that generate income through student fees, research grants, services such as consultancy, and even in some cases philanthropic donations. Do your utmost to maximise these income streams and encourage your staff in all forms of activity and behaviour that contribute to increasing income.

You also need to be aware of the costs of running your unit in all respects. This will naturally include the full staff costs as well as costs of facilities and equipment needed by the unit. In addition, academic units will need to bear some costs of running the university centrally. Such costs will be apportioned according to a formula which may relate to space utilised, numbers of students enrolled, or quantity of research projects undertaken.

Some units in a university will effectively become cost-incurring units without much revenue-generating capability. Not every part of a university can generate income though, with some creative thinking, even cost-incurring units may find a way to generate limited income.

Ultimately, every university needs to be able to generate sufficient income to cover its costs and leave a little leftover as an annual surplus. With the exception of some private-for-profit institutions, most higher education institutions aim to make a small surplus each year of typically around 3%–5% of turnover though sometimes more. This will usually be put aside into a capital reserve fund to support special projects to enhance the institution in subsequent years.

Budgets and Internal "Taxation"

It is essential in any university to set an annual budget which identifies expected income to be generated and the expenditure that can be allowed. This budget will usually be broken down by units or departments and each one should be given a clear and unambiguous description of what is expected in terms of income to be generated (if any) and expenditure that can be permitted, together with the spending pattern through a financial year.

Although it is a matter of contention with some managers, it is a fact of life in universities that those who generate the income do not necessarily get to spend it all. Some departments, schools, or faculties are able to generate a lot more income than others because they have courses which attract more students, or they operate in fields in which it is possible to get more research grants or consultancy income. Consequently, in most institutions, there will be some cross-subsidising going on in which some departments or units are effectively "taxed" to help support others, besides contributing to the general running costs of the institution as a whole.

> **It is a fact of life in universities that those who generate income do not necessarily get to spend it all.**

Central "taxation" is often a matter that gives rise to arguments between middle managers and institutional top-level management. Senior managers must determine how best to deploy financial resources in order to gain maximum benefit for the institution as a whole, according to the priorities set by the governing body. This may involve prioritising certain initiatives, projects, or activities that contribute to institution-building.

Managers of departments or units that generate income may not always perceive priorities in the same way and resent the tax rate applied. It is the duty of a university's president or vice-chancellor to ensure that all members of the institution are aware of the institutional strategic vision and why certain activities are prioritised for funding even if this is a drain on the resources of certain departments.

It is reasonable for healthy debates to take place about budgets and resource disbursement, but ultimately all managers have to take a collegial view and see that the success of the institution as a whole is a higher priority than the financial envelope of their own particular area. Sometimes managers have to accept a less-than-ideal budget to help take the overall institution forward. As a good manager, you accept that and communicate the position clearly to your staff.

Once budgets have been set, it is important for you to monitor regularly the financial position against the budget plan. It is vital to check both the income generation and expenditure month-by-month against the plan. Variances from the plan need to be identified quickly and acted upon, particularly negative variances where income is falling short or expenditure is running ahead of plan.

Failure to rein back expenditure or take action to boost income in negative variance scenarios can soon escalate into a financial crisis, not just for a unit but also for the entire institution. In academia, as in any other field of human activity, finance is king. Without money, institutions can soon be put into a position of reducing staff or cutting back on vital services. A spiral of decline can soon set in if finances are not managed well.

Sometimes you may wish to put forward significant new projects or activities that can potentially generate income as well as incur costs. In all cases of significant activities of such nature, it is essential to do full investment appraisals and business plans. There should be an accurate forecast of the return on investment and the timescales involved. No significant new activity should be embarked upon without such an appraisal. You may need to learn how to produce fully costed business plans and investment appraisals, especially if you have not had the experience of such things before.

One of the major costs of any university will be its staff salaries, which is often the highest cost. Managing the overall salary budget and the compensation and benefits for staff at different grades is a very complex task for management teams to carry out. In public institutions in most countries, staff salaries may be set through nationally negotiated and agreed salary scales. In private institutions or in contexts where there are no national agreements, however, institutions will set salary levels by themselves.

Even if there are broad guidelines at the institutional level, managers usually have some discretion over annual pay rises for individual staff. This discretion has to take into account the annual budget and the overall financial performance of the university. Often, an appraisal scheme will feed into salary increments. Because financial rewards are so sensitive, managers need to ensure that appraisals are done fairly and that outcomes for individuals are not a surprise.

Sometimes universities find themselves in unexpected financial crises because a particular source of income fell short or an unexpected and unavoidable extra expenditure was required. It is in times of financial crisis that managers have to exercise particularly strong management. It may become necessary to cut back on expenditure that many staff would regard as untouchable. In extreme circumstances, it may also become necessary to consider making staff redundant, which is an enormous challenge that requires drawing up terms for redundancy and identifying the criteria for who stays and who goes. There will normally be legal requirements and due process to follow.

Besides managing finances well, most managers in universities also have shared responsibility for generating income. Academic departments will be expected to attract fee-paying students, win research grants, obtain consultancy projects from industry, and run fee-generating conferences or training programmes. In addition, departments and their heads may need to play a role in attracting philanthropic donations, for example by networking with potential donors and sharing with them visions of new opportunities that such donors may wish to invest in. Such opportunities are typically for the benefit of the institution, its students, or humankind more generally (e.g., investment in a research project with significant potential to find a cure a for a particular disease).

Good managers will focus on income generation as a key part of their financial management strategy and will support more senior managers in efforts to raise funds. The very best managers in universities see their roles very much as business unit managers, managing budgets well, and ensuring they divide their efforts between income generation, prudent financial management, and cost control. This is what you should aim to do if you wish to be an exceptionally good academic manager.

CHAPTER 8

Managing Meetings and Communications

The Scourge of Meetings and How to Avoid It

It is an unfortunate fact that a lot of staff in universities seem to spend much of their time in meetings. We can postulate several reasons for this. Firstly, while many academics say they dislike meetings, they mostly enjoy problem-solving and debating ideas, and meetings often involve both. Secondly, because academics have relatively unstructured daily schedules and are not teaching formal classes all of the time, they are actually available for meetings. Thirdly, most staff in universities work there because they enjoy being in an environment that is often seen as being a democratic community of scholars in which key decisions are taken collectively. Most ancient universities were originally monastic or religious communities in which a "collegial" mode of behaviour was often the norm and it seems to have stuck.

Meetings, however, can become a huge time-wasting activity for many staff in universities; effectively they can become a scourge. They can be a big distraction from the core activities of the university. Time spent in meetings debating and arguing over issues is time not spent on teaching, research, supporting students, or other important core activities. As a manager in a university, you have a big responsibility in relation to meetings to ensure that they are productive activities and not distractions.

> **Meetings can become a huge time-wasting activity for many staff in universities; effectively they can become a scourge.**

Managers are normally responsible for convening them and for chairing them. If you call too many and chair them badly, then meetings have the capacity to waste a lot of staff time and reduce the institution's overall effectiveness. More time in meetings also means less time doing the things that really matter to the university's overall standing and reputation. Staff often want to use meetings to decide on important matters but also expect unanimous collegial decisions, which are sometimes difficult or impossible to achieve. This tendency can also prolong meetings unnecessarily.

Some meetings will be called on an ad hoc basis to deal with matters that arise from time to time which need some form of group discussion, consultation, and decision-making. Other meetings will be those of formal committees that have to meet because they are established by the university's constitution or which senior management or the governing body feel are necessary to ensure effective governance and management at a variety of levels.

When it comes to ad hoc meetings, the manager convening them has the key responsibility to determine who should be invited to attend. The manager has to take a balanced view between ensuring that all relevant stakeholders are involved in the discussion and decision-making on the one hand, and ensuring that staff time is not wasted unnecessarily on the other. Getting this right can sometimes be a challenge. With too many invitees staff time may be wasted, but with too few invitees some may feel left out and become resentful that they were not consulted on a matter on which they believe they have something important to contribute.

When it comes to formal committees, the membership is something over which the chair may have less direct control because it may be laid down in the institution's articles of governance, charter, or some other legal framework. Even then, the formal membership usually can be changed by asking a higher body, such as the academic senate or governing body or equivalent senior body, to agree to it. In practice, academic senates or governing bodies would be expected to agree to a change if a good argument is put forward for doing so. So, managers stuck with inordinately unwieldy committees should be able to find a way to optimise the membership for maximum effectiveness.

The other critical issue in the effectiveness of meetings is the way in which it is chaired. The chair needs to ensure that the meeting moves swiftly down the agenda without becoming bogged down at length on certain items. Firstly, if the meeting has formal minutes and is part of a sequence of meetings, it is important not to dwell too long on looking at the minutes of the previous meeting. Otherwise, the current meeting is merely re-running the last one. Minutes of the previous meeting should be opened for amendments by members and then there should be a brief update by members on actions decided last time. This review and update should, in practice, take no more than a few minutes.

Sometimes members may try to keep the discussion going at length about items discussed at the last meeting, but the chair needs to be firm and ensure that only new information is discussed and very briefly, otherwise today's agenda will not be covered. A good chair will strike a balance between reviewing matters arising from the last meeting and ensuring enough time is devoted to the new items on the agenda of the current meeting. A ratio of 10% to 90% would be an appropriate balance. The new items need to have priority.

A good chair will also ensure that the most important items for discussion requiring key decisions will be high on the agenda and not left to the very end. Nothing is worse than spending a lot of time on relatively trivial matters and then running out of time to discuss key matters at the end.

One question that often taxes great minds is how long a meeting should last. It is not uncommon to find meetings in universities lasting several hours, because of the propensity (referred to earlier) of some individuals, especially academics, to debate at length. In practice, few decisions really need prolonged discussions, but a key challenge is bringing matters to a close and ensuring that clear actions, if needed, are determined.

Chairs of meetings should ideally determine to finish them within one hour, or perhaps one-and-a-half hours at most. Achieving this can be a challenge. One way of doing so is to ensure that essential background information is made available to the meeting to allow an informed debate to take place and that the discussion is kept focused. The tendency of some members of a committee to go off on tangents must be resisted by the chair.

Also, the chair needs to bring the meeting to a clear conclusion on each agenda item. The outcome should be completely clear and unambiguous. If necessary, a discussion on a particular topic can be adjourned to a future meeting if more information is needed or persons not present need to be consulted. At all times the manager in the chair role has the responsibility to keep the meeting moving swiftly down the agenda with the aim of finishing the meeting as quickly as possible, but with the key decisions taken and recorded clearly.

If necessary, the chair may need to bring debate on a matter to a conclusion to avoid it dragging on. Having heard a range of views, he or she should summarise what has been said, put forward what he or she thinks is the majority view on the way forward, and ask for the committee's support. Hopefully, nods of assent will be sufficient to signal that the matter can be closed and the meeting can move on to the next item.

Very rarely, if the matter is highly contentious and there does not seem to be a consensus view, it may be necessary to ask the meeting to vote on an outcome. This should be avoided, if possible, as this is an admission that a consensus cannot be achieved and the will of the majority is determined to prevail.

As a means of minimising the need for formally convened meetings, I very much advocate daily informal social gatherings of staff, such as for morning coffee, as a means of getting a lot of minor business issues settled easily without convening a meeting. This was a practice I observed, and participated in, as a young doctoral student in Oxford. Our entire department, or whoever was available, gathered in a rooftop coffee lounge at 11 am each day to catch up on news, both social- and work-related. It worked well as a means of building a good team spirit and of solving minor problems over some refreshment.

I also saw it later when I was a lecturer in a UK university where the academics and department head would come together in a coffee room at the same time each morning. Such brief 15-minute communal refreshment breaks enable a lot of issues to be discussed and resolved without needing to schedule something more formal and disruptive.

Being a Good Communicator

Besides handling meetings and committees well, becoming a good manager in academia—especially a great manager—really does require you to be a good communicator in multiple contexts. This means being good at handling email or other forms of electronic communication including social media, doing good presentations, and writing good reports.

All managers these days need to be highly sensitive to the fact that most people in universities are overloaded with communications of various kinds; some might even go as far as to say they are "drowning" in communications besides meetings. It is a reality of 21st-century business life that many emails go unopened, many documents are skim-read. In such a context, a good manager needs to understand this reality, keep it constantly in mind, and adapt his or her behaviour accordingly.

So, what does this mean in practice for a good university manager? Firstly, it is important to keep email communications to the minimum, both in terms of the number of messages and the length of them. As a manager, whenever you send someone an email you should immediately ask yourself two questions: (a) how can I make this really short? and (b) to whom am I going to send this? The best emails are only one or two sentences long and sent to just one person. Sometimes there will be a need to send a copy to a second person, but above all, avoid the tendency to send long, rambling emails and copies to a lot of people unless there are really compelling reasons to do so.

In most cases, email messages are intended for one person to read and to act on or respond to. If you are the sender, is it then really necessary to let many other people know that you have sent it to the recipient? Also, is it really necessary to go into issues in great length? Some may appreciate being kept informed about what you are saying to other people, but many will dislike you for cluttering up their inboxes with things they do not feel they need to know about.

In fact, including many recipients in a "cc" list and writing long messages may soon generate some hostility towards you, especially if the recipients view the messages as having little to do with them. You are effectively intruding on their busy day with your thoughts directed at someone else.

Apart from minimising messages, a good university manager takes great care with the tone of electronic communications. Emails or social media interventions should be polite and business-like and generally friendly, but not overly so. Emails should not be used as a replacement for face-to-face conversations. If the recipient is in a nearby office and can be spoken to more rapidly than typing and sending an email, then just speak do not type! Face-to-face communication is both friendlier and more effective.

Face-to-face communication allows you to convey information more effectively through non-verbal cues and also allows you to sense and judge the emotions of the person with whom you are communicating. We have already looked at the role of EI in good management and it is therefore imperative to use a method of communication that maximises the communication of emotions.

One of the main problems with electronic communication is that it is usually difficult to detect subtleties in emotions. Extreme emotions usually show through, such as anger, but subtle ones do not. Sometimes the emotions can be miscommunicated or misunderstood in electronic written communications. There can also be a tendency to say things more directly and forcefully in electronic communications than face-to-face interactions. This can soon lead to bad feelings between colleagues.

A simple sentence spoken with a smile can be interpreted very differently to the same sentence read from an email message where the smile is not present. A friendly request to do something may sound like a formal order when converted into the cold black text of an email. Good managers in universities need to be very sensitive to this at all times.

> **One of the main problems with electronic communication is that extreme emotions usually show through, but subtle ones do not.**

One of the most important lessons for new managers in relation to emails is never to react quickly to messages that you find annoying or troublesome. If someone has sent you an email in which he or she has challenged you, expressed anger towards you, or tried to humiliate you in front of others (through an extended "cc" list), do not under any circumstances reply immediately. If you reply straightaway your mind will be full of emotion and you are likely to say something that will just fuel an email war.

> **Never react quickly to messages that you find annoying or troublesome.**

If you sit on a hostile email overnight without replying, your reaction to it the next day will be much milder. You will no longer be so emotional about it, as the initial shock of it will have gone away. When you have had a chance to sleep on it, you will get it more into perspective and realise that it does not actually mean very much in the grand scheme of things. You will then be able to send a carefully crafted neutral reply and defuse what otherwise could have become an escalating war of words. Even better, arrange a face-to-face meeting to defuse the issue.

Remember, as we have discussed previously, being a good manager in a university means maintaining a calm and peaceful working environment and maximising happiness to achieve good productive outcomes. You will find yourself on occasions having to ignore challenges, insults, and threats coming in the form of emails and keep your eye firmly fixed on what needs to be done to maintain a happy and productive working environment.

Becoming immune to provocation is a key requirement of a good manager, and particularly of a great manager in a university, and will usually result in respect and appreciation. Even your attackers may come to respect you if they see that their electronic attacks are not met with counterattacks but instead with friendly business-focused communications. Usually, of course, they never intended to "attack" you in the first place; they were feeling quite emotional about something when they crafted a message to you and the moderation that normally occurs in a face-to-face conversation (except in some extreme situations) was lost. Sometimes attacks can be intentional and amount to cyberbullying. It is always best simply not to react to any attack that is tantamount to cyberbullying.

Apart from mastering the complexities and emotional aspects of emails, it is also very important for university managers to understand a few key principles in regard to reports, business plans, policy documents, and other forms of written business communication. All managers have to produce written business documents quite frequently, which can serve many purposes and may be directed at a variety of audiences. There are some important lessons to be learnt early on if you wish to be seen as a competent manager.

The most important of all is to keep them brief, just as we said about emails. No one likes to read through massive documents. We are all too busy to sit down and read through them. Business documents need to be short, well-structured, and make good use of graphics such as diagrams or graphs to convey key messages.

They also need to be perfect without errors. Any errors suggest to the reader either that you are incompetent and lack the ability to spell correctly or write grammatically or, alternatively, that you are sloppy in your work and too lazy to check over what you have written. Neither conveys a good message about you. So, make sure your documents are 100% correct before sending them to others.

If you are preparing a document for a more senior manager, you should keep it as short as possible. If you are preparing one that will be read by the most senior managers in your institution, such as the president or vice-chancellor, you should make them very short indeed.

Top managers rarely have time to read anything longer than two pages at most. You need to distil the key elements of what you want to say into as little text as possible. You have to work out what essential messages you want to put over with as little padding as possible. Just get to the key conclusions or recommendations as quickly as possible with a minimal amount of background explanation. If it is absolutely necessary to produce a long document, then it is best to produce a one- or two-page "executive summary" that is put at the beginning of the document. It is likely that most senior managers will get no further than your summary.

Besides written communications, good managers will frequently be communicating with their staff and other audiences orally through presentations and speeches. A manager needs to develop the skills to handle these various situations and to give a good impression at all times.

For many academic managers, the skill of doing good presentations comes naturally because of their background in teaching, but not to all. The most important thing to remember about presentations is to keep to time. Presentations that take too long become annoying for the audience or send them to sleep.

Also, always ensure your presentations give a clear message and reach an unambiguous conclusion. You are using the presentation to convey some new ideas or messages to others and it is essential that they go away enlightened with new information or ideas that have been clearly expressed. Sometimes you may have to give a presentation to a very important audience, such as the institution's top-level management or governing board, or perhaps to visiting dignitaries or industrialists. The more important or the larger the audience, the more necessary it becomes to put in the effort to perfect the performance.

Finally, apart from presentations, you will often find yourself as a manager giving speeches. These are also an important part of managerial communication in any organisation, including universities. Sometimes speeches will be formal, for example on special occasions such as the opening of a new facility. Other times they will be informal or impromptu, such as at a leaving party for a member of staff.

Clearly, the formal ones need to be prepared well in advance and delivered with confidence and an appropriate level of seriousness. Your audience will expect you to say something appropriate to the occasion. The more informal ones should also be taken seriously, and again, you need to say something appropriate. Your staff will look to you to say something at key moments such as a member of staff leaving. On these occasions, you will be the spokesperson for your team and have to reflect their sentiments and possible sadness at losing a valued colleague who is moving on.

How you handle such occasions can reinforce the confidence that your staff feel in you. You need to get the mood right and ensure that everyone involved goes away with a good feeling afterwards. It can take time to get accustomed to how to handle these informal events, but nonetheless learning to handle them well is a key part of learning how to be a good manager in higher education, as in any other industry.

CHAPTER 9

Engaging Support Services

Although the core business of a university or other higher education institution is educating students, undertaking research, and transferring knowledge to industry, none of this happens without a wide range of support services that take place behind the scenes. The support services typically include Human Resources (HR), Finance, Student Welfare Services, Accommodation Services, Student Records and Registry Services, Library and Information Services, Marketing and Public Relations (PR) Services, Careers Services, Estates and Facilities, Information and Communication Technology (ICT) Services, Planning, Partnerships Management, Alumni Support, Fundraising and Development, Research Grant Support Services, etc. These support services are as essential to the functioning of a university and the delivery of its mission as any other part of the institution. As an academic manager, you have to ensure that you interact effectively with such support services and with the operational managers who lead them.

A common issue in many institutions is lack of mutual respect or understanding between academic staff delivering the core teaching, research, and knowledge transfer missions and the support service staff who provide all the background functions that support those missions. This lack of respect often comes about because some academics, who are highly expert in their fields, consider themselves to be more valuable to their institutions than support service staff members, who may not be as highly qualified academically or as rare in terms of expertise or experience.

In reality, everyone deserves respect and is equally important in enabling the institution to achieve its goals. A stellar soccer team cannot win a match if the groundsmen or women have not prepared a high-quality pitch.

Managers of support services are generally highly educated and well-trained for their roles just like academics, but the qualifications needed are usually professional ones in fields such as accountancy, estate management, hospitality, law, or public administration. Sometimes, individuals who have entered universities as academics transfer into roles where they are no longer academics and instead manage a support service. Moreover, managers in universities may sometimes even be called upon to manage both an academic area as well as a support service department, so the division between "academic" managers and "non-academic" managers is not always clear. The boundary can be fuzzy or porous.

Even so, there is often an unhelpful separation between categories of staff that does not always contribute towards institutional harmony. For example, academics often get more generous leave allowances than non-academics, based on a long-standing perception that academics work very hard during semester time and need time to refresh when the semester is over. In reality, most committed staff in contemporary higher education institutions, whether academic or non-academic, work hard all year round and distinctions between categories of staff and their compensation and benefits are arguably antiquated, particularly for those with equal years of training and experience.

Managing support services can, therefore, be challenging in any university. Support service managers often need to strive to promote their services and to get noticed and taken seriously by academics. It can take a certain degree of resilience and hard-headedness to handle what can be a condescending attitude of some academics towards the support services and their managers.

What is most essential is that both academic and support service managers buy into the institutional long-term strategy, which is most likely to have a strong academic focus, and ensure that they are delivering high-quality professional services to support its achievement in partnership. The need for a good working relationship is paramount and academic managers need to make it a key priority to respect operational support managers and build a good rapport with them and vice versa.

Support services, just like academic departments, provide student-facing services and need to be adept at handling the student body and ensuring their services are efficient and courteous. Ineffective, incompetent, or inadequate support services can impact significantly on student perceptions of their institution and can damage the reputation of a university that, in terms of its academic quality, may be excellent or outstanding.

As such, academic managers should collaborate with support service managers in ensuring that customer-facing engagements are of high quality and that there is a shared culture of continuous improvement with both sides helping one another. Academic managers can often learn from support services and should value them as equal contributors to the institution's mission.

> **Academic managers have to ensure that they interact effectively with support services and with the operational managers who lead them.**

Increasingly, support services in a university context are delivered as e-services just as teaching can be increasingly delivered online. There is much scope for academic and support functions to collaborate on using electronic platforms with the aim of harmonising or integrating their various "customer" interactions.

In some institutions, there is scope for use of shared services, which can improve overall efficiency. This can happen when certain support services can be shared between a university and one or more other entities, such as other educational institutions in a group or system structure, or perhaps between a university and a parent company in a private education context, or between a university and another body such as a hospital in a public context. Shared support services can provide some efficiencies through economies of scale.

However, they are not problem-free. In some cases, it can be difficult to provide shared services which adapt well to the different needs of the various institutions or entities that are sharing them. Practices and processes that work well for one may not necessarily work well for all. Managing the variety of needs can be a problem for support service managers and there may be a need for regular reviews of service effectiveness and a willingness to engage in process re-engineering if found to be necessary.

Academic managers need to understand the context in which their institutional support services are being delivered and, in particular, to understand the constraints within which their support service colleagues are operating. Ultimately, improved understanding can lead to a stronger partnership and close collaboration in ensuring that the institution works exceedingly well as a whole and offers outstanding service to its stakeholders.

In my personal view, some academic managers are not easily approachable and can appear intimidating to some support service managers. In the true spirit of working together for institutional development, it really is necessary for academic managers to go out of their way to engage in a highly positive and constructive manner with support service managers and to share ideas on service improvement. Sharing should be polite and respectful, not arrogant and demanding; something I have seen all too often.

To minimise cost, some universities have taken the route of outsourcing certain support services to external service providers. There is an increasing trend towards this, particularly in regard to cloud-based ICT services, but even other forms of support service can be outsourced. Outsourcing can be contentious and there are certainly pros and cons.

On the plus side, there is an opportunity for a university to reduce the support service staff headcount and to operate a service that is at a higher level of professionalism because it is undertaken by a specialist company. On the negative side, there may be less control of the service and its costs, and it may not be tailored sufficiently to the precise needs of the university. To be sure of getting the right kind of service quality, a service level agreement (SLA) should be negotiated and agreed with the outsourcing provider.

Regardless of whether in-house services, shared services, or outsourced services are used, fundamentally the support service delivery has to be effective, of high quality, and integrated with the academic endeavours of the institution. A key point is that managers of professional support services have to be aware of the academic needs of the institution and adapt their services to the changing nature of the institution as a whole. As universities evolve academically, so must their support services.

Whether it is to support more academic departments and courses, more students, a larger real estate base, a growing staff base, or demands from students for better facilities, the support services have to grow in response to the growth of the institution. A support service designed for an institution of 3,000 students will need to evolve significantly if the institution grows to 10,000 students. Processes that worked for 3,000 may be far too slow once the student number reaches 10,000, and may effectively grind to a halt once the student body reaches 20,000.

However, managers of support services can only expand and upgrade their services to meet increased requirements if the academic managers share their ideas on academic developments with them. This comes back to the absolute necessity of working closely together and ensuring all parts of an institution pull together.

Most institutions will ensure that there is an appropriate management forum for both academic managers and support service managers to come together to ensure the effectiveness of the institution's day-to-day activities as well as its long-term success. Whether or not such a forum exists formally, it is essential that academic and support service managers work collaboratively on taking an institution forward with academic managers going out of their way to engage with their support service colleagues.

CHAPTER 10

Managing with Analytics

Using KPIs to Drive Development

The ability to take sensible well-balanced decisions in regard to institutional development is the hallmark of a good manager. Bad decision-makers usually find their managerial careers relatively short-lived. Universities need high-quality decision-making and to move forward on the basis of actions guided by clear evidence and core data on performance in many aspects of their activities.

Universities can and should manage their performance using a range of key performance indicators (KPIs). These KPIs will relate to the core missions of the institution and may be analysed at varying levels of granularity depending on what priorities are given to particular areas for development. KPIs may also be monitored at the overall institutional level or at a subsidiary level, such as by department, faculty, or school. Typical KPIs would be:

- total number of student applicants and proportion accepted, their origins, school grades, and changes in such figures year by year;

- total number of students, proportion of students in categories such as gender, ethnicity, socioeconomic background, etc., and changes in such data year by year;
- income and expenditure versus budget and surplus/loss position, as well as other accounting information such as the balance sheet;
- student outcomes in terms of number attaining high honours classes, proportion employed within N months of course completion, average salary obtained in first job post-graduation, percentage progressing to graduate study, and percentage starting their own businesses (as students or upon graduation);
- student retention in terms of percentage successfully progressing from one year of a programme to the next and the percentage ultimately completing their programme successfully;
- research outcomes in terms of number of successful research grant applications, research income obtained annually, number of research papers published per year in total and in specific categories of publications (e.g., tier 1 academic journals), citations generated per year, and number or proportion of successful research degree completions;
- outcomes from engagements with industry in terms of number of industry-linked projects, income received from consultancy or applied research, number of patents applied for and/or granted, and income received from exploitation of IP;

- outcomes from engagements with the global academic community such as number of staff engaged as peer-reviewed academic journal editors, as conference chairs, or as members of major grant assessing committees;
- indicators of effectiveness in engagement with their local community such as spending on charitable activities, number of community events hosted on campus, number of stories generated in local media, etc.; and
- overall indicators of global effectiveness, recognition, and influence, such as worldwide institutional ranking, regional rankings, subject-specific rankings, web-based rankings, number of staff winning major academic awards or prizes, and number of national or international media stories about the institution.

Clearly, there are dozens, if not hundreds, of measures derived from the aforementioned that can be used to monitor the performance of an institution overall as well as of its subsidiary components. Most institutions will have a corporate planning department that will generate the relevant KPIs deemed critical in the evaluation of the institution's progress towards its overall strategic objectives. As an academic manager, you need to be aware

> **Universities need high-quality decision-making and to move forward on the basis of actions guided by clear evidence and data.**

of the KPIs applying to your part of the organisation as a whole and to ensure, as part of good management, that those KPIs are trending in the right direction.

Using Analytics

No manager in contemporary higher education can ignore the fact that we live in an era of big data and data analytics. Most institutions have vast quantities of data on their activities and on their students and other stakeholders. These data can be very valuable and informative if analysed appropriately and presented in ways to show how the institution is evolving as well as to identify new opportunities.

Good university managers, therefore, embrace data analytics and use data visualisation and graphics to communicate how the institution or a specific department is doing. This might encompass the following types of data and analytics (not an exhaustive list, and subject always to data protection or privacy laws):

- Marketing analytics: Using data gathered from potential student applicants and enquirers to identify patterns in applicants, their likelihood of joining the institution, and potential for successful completion of their programmes
- Student performance analytics: Using data on student performance across a wide variety of activities to identify those who are at risk of non-

completion or of dropping out and planning appropriate intervention strategies

- HR analytics: Using data on personnel and applicants for employment to determine those who are most likely to be successful future employees and those who should be fast-tracked for training programmes and promotion
- Research analytics: Using data on multiple aspects of research performance to determine research spending priorities, the optimum channels for seeking external research grants, and to predict likely returns on future major research investments
- Social media analytics: Using data on any sentiment expressed about the institution on social media to identify student experience issues that may need to be addressed or to respond to trending stories about the institution that may need to be amplified or countered to boost or protect its reputation

In the highly competitive world of higher education, those institutions that use KPIs and data analytics most effectively are likely to gain an advantage over their less analytical competitors. Not every manager necessarily needs to be fully acquainted with data analytics tools, but most need to work with those who can use such tools to extract the most meaningful data in terms of how the university needs to evolve.

Crystallising data into relevant charts is a key requirement for most managers in higher education. Such charts can become the key medium of communication with teams about performance, strengths, and weaknesses. Charts might include "dashboards" showing dials or gauges for KPIs, or perhaps "traffic light diagrams" where KPIs get colour-coded depending on how well the institution or department is doing (green = ok, orange = needs improvement, red = problem area needing to be urgently addressed).

Graphical representation of performance can be one of the most effective tools for a manager to drive change in a university, as the picture can distil an extremely complex situation into a relatively comprehensible product that all staff can relate to. The power of using graphical representations should not be underestimated— as is often said, a picture is worth a thousand words.

> **Institutions that use KPIs and data analytics most effectively are likely to gain an advantage over their less analytical competitors.**

We should also recognise that institutional development may need to be driven by non-quantitative factors. Not everything can be expressed as numerical goals or easily measured by quantitative KPIs. For example, there may be an aspiration to change the culture of an institution, but measuring exactly what the culture is now and whether progress has been made towards a new culture may be difficult to do in a quantitative way.

Yet even intangible concepts, such as staff or student contentment, may be assessed through analytics applied to sentiments expressed on social media. Increasingly, as technology is used for both formal and informal communication, the power of data analytics to understand how an institution is progressing and what stakeholders of all types think about it becomes ever stronger.

CHAPTER 11

Decisions, Risks, and Crises

Decision-Making in Challenging Circumstances

We have seen that the ability to make good decisions is characteristic of a good manager and that these decisions can often be informed by data and evidence. Sometimes, however, decisions will need to be taken in the context of challenging circumstances or crises, which can be particularly difficult for any manager to handle. You may have to take them quickly in the absence of complete information. Crises are often less serious if good risk management has been exercised before such crises occur. Managing risks, handling crises, and making complex decisions are therefore interrelated and worth some discussion.

In the university context, you would think that managers are not likely to make totally bad decisions because they are used to evidence-based analysis and reasoning. The critical appraisal of arguments and the analysis of data and evidence are key skills of academics that they themselves master and pass on to their students. However, even though they may have the skills and ability to make careful decisions, it is surprising how often managers in universities seem to get decisions very wrong.

Why is this? One line of argument is that most managerial decisions that matter are decisions relating to human problems which academics are not, as a whole, particularly good at because they spend too much time thinking about abstract problems in their research and teaching. This, of course, is a simplistic and almost certainly misguided view, but there is little doubt that some academics may have had too little experience of solving human problems as they climbed the academic career hierarchy and may well lack exposure to human problems that need common-sense human decisions.

Many decisions that you make daily, as a higher education manager, will indeed be related to simple human problems and may have to be taken relatively quickly on the basis of limited or incomplete information. These can be quite different to the strategic decisions concerning future direction and development, which may be relatively slow and based on complex data analytics discussed previously. As universities are large communities of scholars, some decisions can have an impact on large numbers of people, which makes it all the more important that they are taken well.

Complex Grading Decisions

To do their job well, university managers need to be able to make good decisions whether or not they have had much experience of doing so. It is not always easy to determine what is or is not a good decision, but often it comes down to natural justice or what is in the interest of the largest number of people. Decisions that go against natural justice or seem to favour a small number of people over others are likely to be bad ones. Some of the most difficult decisions for managers to make in the university context relate to students, so let us consider a typical, highly challenging decision-making scenario.

When students receive their final results at the end of their programmes, there will always be some whose numerical results put them just below a boundary for a particular honours class. Such students may feel aggrieved that they have just missed the higher class by a narrow margin.

Decisions that go against natural justice or seem to favour a small number of people over others are likely to be bad ones.

Given that the final honours class of their degree can determine their prospects for obtaining high-quality employment or places on highly competitive postgraduate programmes, the desire to achieve the "just missed" honours class can be very strong. This may result in academic appeals being submitted to the university right after final results are announced. In such appeals, students will claim a right to the higher class on a variety of grounds, typically including unfairness in the assessment process, inadequate teaching or support by the university, or personal problems such as health issues.

Even though universities will normally have strict rules encapsulated within their regulations on what grounds students may lodge academic appeals, it is nonetheless common for students not to follow such rules and to make challenges on grounds that they see fit, with threats of legal action in some cases if their appeal is not considered.

As the stakes can be so high for the student(s) concerned, so is the pressure to appeal and achieve a satisfactory outcome in terms of an honours class upgrade. Students, their parents, and even their legal representatives can be very forceful and become a real challenge for programme leaders, department heads, deans, and even presidents or vice-chancellors to manage.

This problem has been growing in severity as students increasingly see themselves as high fee-paying customers in many countries who expect a good result and excellent career opportunities as a result of their considerable investment of time and money in obtaining a degree. Despite the increasingly difficult challenge posed to academic managers and administrators, this problem has received little attention in the higher education literature. Yet it can be a huge burden to staff and often places them in a position of conflict with their former students. At a time when staff and students should be celebrating the latter's achievement, an atmosphere of enmity and confrontation can occur, damaging a relationship that has been built up over several years.

The problem with many situations like this is that universities operate with rules and regulations and try to enforce them or obey them very strictly. Academics will say that is what the rules are for. Yet, in fact, the rules and regulations that universities develop for themselves are like the laws of nations—they are sometimes broken and sometimes things happen that exist in a grey area. That is why nations have courts and judges to make decisions about matters that may not be entirely clear under the rule of law.

University managers will thus sometimes find themselves having to behave like judges, trying to come to the right decision when matters are not entirely clear-cut. In the case of the student who misses a first-class degree by just 1%, the manager has to decide whether the student's appeal against the second-class degree result has any validity. A student may well argue that the staff of the university cannot mark pieces of his or her work within an accuracy of 1%. With the possible exception of some highly formulaic or mathematical assessments, this is almost certainly true. Most assessments that take place in universities are partially subjective. Academics have to make subjective assessments of essays and other outputs produced by students.

Certainly, systems and mechanisms, such as model marking schemes, will have been put in place to ensure as much objectivity as possible, but some subjectivity will still remain. It is effectively impossible to remove subjectivity in all forms of student assessment. In this regard, the student's argument that the university could not assess his or her work within a tolerance band of 1% is almost certainly going to be correct, at least on face value.

So, what is the academic manager, dean, or department head going to do in this situation? The answer, as always, is to make a sensible decision based on natural justice and common sense. It would not be appropriate to raise this student's degree class result simply because he or she appealed and pointed out that it is impossible to mark accurately assessments within 1%.

This is because the degree result is an accumulation of many assessment marks and it is just as likely that some assessments will have been graded generously as others have been graded ungenerously along the way. Also, simply raising the degree result of one student who is so close to the borderline will not do justice to other students who are also equally close to a degree class borderline. Academics will often argue against reconsidering the results of a borderline student for fear of "opening the floodgates" to other students.

The correct approach in this case, is for the academic manager to behave like a judge and do his or her best to make a well-balanced decision. That means justice for the student in question and justice for all other students of that particular degree programme as well as of the wider university.

You need to consider as much evidence as possible that relates to the student's case. You need to ask whether or not this student was disadvantaged in any way compared to other students by factors outside of his or her control, for example, a period of significant illness, when undertaking the programme. Alternatively, it is necessary to consider whether there are any special circumstances that make this student different from other borderline candidates.

If there are such special circumstances, it may then be appropriate to raise the student's degree class result because of natural justice. Before doing so, however, it is important for the manager concerned to get advice and buy-in from others. Difficult decisions such as this should not be taken by one individual without seeking views. Such views should ideally come from highly experienced managers at the same or a higher level. Ideally, such views should come from managers outside of the department or faculty who will have a more detached and hopefully objective view of the situation; where external examiners are appointed from other universities they should normally be asked to contribute their views. As in many aspects of academic life, peer views and opinions are extremely important.

Scenarios such as the one described demonstrate just how difficult it can be for managers in universities to take what should, on the face of it, be simple decisions. Many matters requiring decisions that come onto the desks of academic managers will be equally difficult. Above all, a good manager will look at the problem in

> **A zealous reliance on institutional rules and regulations will not always yield an answer which conforms to natural justice.**

the round, examining all aspects of the problem and working towards a decision of natural justice based on relevant evidence. A zealous reliance on institutional rules and regulations will not always yield an answer which conforms to natural justice.

The Acceptability of U-Turns

One further issue to consider in decision-making is whether it is ever appropriate to do a "U-turn"—in other words, to go back on a decision and to change direction after the decision has been taken. U-turns are generally unhelpful because they can indicate that a decision was badly taken in the first instance. They can also be a sign of weakness in cultures where university leaders or managers are expected to be firm, resolute, and worthy of great respect for taking the correct decisions.

Yet managers should not hesitate to perform a U-turn, if it turns out, perhaps on the basis of new evidence or factors previously unconsidered, that the initial decision was wrong. It is imperative to get to the right outcome consistent with common sense and natural justice even if that means that a decision has to be changed.

Understandably, changing decisions can cause considerable difficulties if the original decision has put actions in motion that are difficult to undo. In such cases, it may be better to live with the poor decision as long as it is not going to do significant damage to the institution or individuals. Weighing up when it is or is not appropriate to change a decision can in itself be a challenging decision, but that is what managers are essentially paid for. Nothing can ever be decided or determined 100% correctly all of the time. Any manager in a university needs to appreciate this, even though it may go against his or her rational academic instincts.

Risk Management

Like many complex organisations, universities have to manage a variety of risks that can have a significant impact on their activities and reputation. These risks can include many things, but typical ones are loss of revenue streams, potential downturn in student recruitment, damage to real estate or critical infrastructure, student dissatisfaction and unrest, staff disquiet and strikes, regulatory infractions that result in penalties or reputation damage, highly negative social media stories, and other forms of disruptive or damaging occurrences.

Most good universities have a risk management process in place so that risks are routinely evaluated, mitigating measures are put in place and regularly reviewed, and any remedial actions needed to deal with urgent and growing risks are taken. Risk management needs to involve managers at all levels, and there should be risk registers of perceived risks, their likelihood, and their impact maintained at all levels and by all institutional units, including academic departments, schools and faculties, and support service areas. Each will have a different view of the major risks and needs for mitigating them.

Risks that have a high likelihood of occurring as well as high impact should be regarded as the most severe and require risk mitigation measures to be put in place within a short timescale. All managers operating in a university need to be familiar with their institution's approach to risk management and do their part in ensuring their area of responsibility plays its full role in managing risks of all kinds envisaged.

Crises

Most universities will from time to time experience crises that test the skills of their managers and leaders to the utmost. As organisations with thousands of employees and students, highly complex activities, and often large amounts of real estate, residences, and infrastructure, there is plenty of scope for crises to occur. Crisis events can take many forms, but what makes them crises is that they are unexpected, may threaten normal daily operations or activities in a significant way, or give rise to significant negative publicity which could affect the long-term reputation of the institution. Often, all three aspects occur together.

Crises come in many forms and it is therefore impossible to name every kind of crisis that can occur in a university. Typical ones are major fires; serious crimes committed on campus; student suicides or other unexpected student deaths perhaps from drug overdoses, accidents, or initiation rites that go badly wrong; outbreaks of epidemics in student residences; involvement of students in terrorism; a major loss of or disruption to IT systems (with potential destruction of vital data); a significant level of student unrest or protests; and mass academic cheating events. Such occurrences, though rare, are all possible in almost any higher education institution and require careful and appropriate management. The global coronavirus disease (COVID-19) pandemic of 2020 is a crisis that was unforeseen yet had a massive effect on higher education globally, affecting flows of international students and requiring many institutions to rapidly switch to delivering teaching and learning solely online.[18]

Crises can place enormous mental stress on university management as well as on front-line student-facing staff. Crises may sometimes be limited to one part of the institution and be relatively contained, but on other occasions may involve or affect the whole organisation, or even affect entire higher education systems of nations as happened with the COVID-19 pandemic.

Crises can, of course, be very disturbing for the managers involved. Individuals who have been promoted into managerial or leadership positions because of their academic track records and intellectual abilities may have little idea of how to face and manage a crisis. Being aware of what crises can occur and thinking ahead about how you might react and deal with them can be helpful.

Ideally, a good institution will prepare crisis management procedures and operating manuals, and ensure that key managers are trained on them. Preparation on the off-chance of something serious happening is far better than making it all up for the first time on the day. Crisis management procedures need to identify the responsibilities of individual managers as well as how they will be contacted and how they will stay in communication with each other, as a team, as the crisis develops and is resolved.

The main priorities in a crisis are firstly, to understand the nature of the crisis and its likely impact; secondly, to bring it under control and minimise organisational or human impact; thirdly, to manage the PR aspect and communications with the university community, stakeholders, emergency services, and the wider public or news media; and fourthly, to put in place remedial actions to try to prevent such a crisis from happening again. Each one of these can involve a complex set of activities and require managers to use a wide range of skills that they rarely get to exercise.

Typically, university managers will be quite skilled at rational thinking, logically analysing what happened and determining how to proceed to minimise impact and take corrective action. However, what can often be most challenging for university managers is the unpredictability of how events unfold, the unexpected reactions of some stakeholders which may be highly emotional, a possible media barrage, and the difficulty of managing communications effectively to stop unwarranted public criticism, reputational damage, or even outright hostility towards the institution or its managers and leaders.

Any university facing a newly developing crisis must of course act in the first instance to contain it and reduce its impact through preserving life, infrastructure, or reputation, depending on the nature of the crisis. After that, the major factor determining the overall impact of the crisis organisationally is the effectiveness of the communications. Managers need to determine who needs to be communicated with and what is to be said by whom, when, and through what medium. Ideally, communications need to be carefully planned by a crisis management team which involves all relevant managers.

In such circumstances, any university manager involved in dealing with the situation is likely to be under severe stress and having to confront significant animosity.

It is very difficult for any university manager to prepare for this, but through planning the communications carefully with a team of colleagues who share in managing the crisis, some of the pressure can be reduced. Again, it is absolutely necessary to use EI in such sensitive crisis situations.

Communications with other stakeholders and the wider public through the media also have to be handled very carefully. These communications need to be managed by the whole crisis management team so that everyone agrees exactly what will be communicated and when. This takes considerable skill and judgement to get right. Rumours about a crisis can spread very rapidly via social media and inaccurate information may soon spread far and wide.

Communications, therefore, have to be planned as soon as the crisis has developed and will usually need to be phased. At each stage, the communication needs to give accurate information and provide sufficient detail to avoid any unnecessary speculation as to what happened, but not so much detail that it can be insensitive to those most affected by it or prejudice any subsequent investigation. Careful judgement will also be needed to determine when enough has been said through various media channels and if it is time to cease any further communication and to try to close off the crisis situation.

CHAPTER 12

Structures, Ambitions, and Rankings

Academic Structures

Each higher education institution in the world is unique and differs in terms of its academic scope. In simple terms, a university or similar institution is characterised by its academic areas of teaching and research, and how they are structured and presented to the outside world, and by the people who lead it and carry out its academic activity.

Many institutions are broad-based with a wide range of departments spanning the arts and sciences. Others may be narrower, for example focusing primarily on specific disciplines such as the arts (e.g., the Royal College of Arts London), sciences (e.g., Imperial College London), business and economics (e.g., the London School of Economics and Political Science), or health (e.g., the London School of Hygiene and Tropical Medicine).

Managing a university strategically involves putting in place the right structures and the right people to achieve the institution's overall mission and to achieve the specific objectives and goals as laid down by the governing body in the strategic plan over a specified time period, such as five years. The leaders need to be the right ones to drive institutional development. Ideally, they should operate entrepreneurially and be ambitious for the institution. The academic areas need to have contemporary relevance to society and industry, and the structure of the institution needs to give the key academic areas high visibility to the outside world.

As an academic manager, you need to contribute to the long-term development of your institution. It may not be obvious that this is a key part of your job, but it is something to be mindful of. Managers at all levels need to participate in building the institution. Essentially the strategic development involves building the institution structurally, adding new components as it expands, and building the quality, reputation, and visibility of each part of the institution such that it gains in terms of rankings or ratings by external agencies.

Being a good manager will mean managing your own part of the overall institutional structure as well as driving or assisting in the creation of new parts of the structure, or facilitating some reorganisation of the overall structure as and when needed. Although institutions are not defined solely by their structure, individual elements in the structure—such as departments or research institutes— can become both well-known and highly regarded, and boost the overall reputation of the university.

The typical structural elements of most universities in the world are the faculties, schools, departments, institutes, colleges, research centres, research units, and research groups in some shape or form. The components of the structure may be defined in the university's charter or articles of governance or left to the governing body or academic senate to determine.

A typical university may consist of a small number of faculties, each divided into a number of departments. This can be a fairly shallow but broad structure (effectively only two levels deep). A deeper structure would be one that has faculties divided into schools, each of which is then divided into departments. There may then be research centres or groups alongside or within departments that can make the structure even deeper.

> **Managers have to drive the creation of new entities such as institutes and research centres as an institution evolves.**

Normally the structure reflects academic discipline divisions, with cognate subject departments linked together in the same school or faculty. Sometimes, however, this discipline-based structure is supplemented, or even replaced, by cross-disciplinary structures. A graduate school would be a good example of this. Some graduate schools are established to support postgraduate students regardless of their subject of study, although others are subject-specific. Undergraduate colleges supporting undergraduate students may sometimes be cross-disciplinary. In other institutions, they may be subject-specific.

Although the types of components may be fixed for some years, the actual numbers of each structural component (e.g., the number of departments) may change quite frequently. This is because the structure has to reflect the core academic activities which change with time. Sometimes new discipline areas will be introduced requiring a new department.

In other cases, an existing department may become too big and needs to be divided into two. Sometimes two departments shrink and are sufficiently related academically to be merged. The creation, closure, merging, and splitting of components is a common activity in universities and reflects the dynamic evolution of the institution. Universities are rarely static entities.

Most academic managers in a university will effectively have control over one component in the structure. This may be a relatively small component such as a research group at the bottom of the organisational hierarchy, or a large component such as a faculty at the top of the hierarchy, which is itself divided into many sub-components.

It is important to recognise that the structure can be important in determining the overall effectiveness of the organisation. Universities can and do function perfectly well with a wide range of structures. What is most important, however, is that the structure, whatever it is in a particular university, works well. It is a key requirement of management to ensure that the structure works and is fit for purpose. So, what determines whether a structure works well or not? There are many factors at play in relation to this.

Firstly, do the students understand which part of the structure "owns" them and do they feel a sense of belonging and attachment to it? If they do feel a strong affinity to a particular component within the structure, such as a department or school, they are more likely to have a better overall student experience as they will relate to other students affiliated to the same component. They will also more easily identify with the staff members who are also part of that component of the institution.

Secondly, do the academic staff members themselves clearly understand which part of the structure they belong to? Do they feel they really belong there? Does the structure make sense to them? Do the individual staff members feel that the structure brings them closer to colleagues who share common academic interests and teach or research similar subjects? Staff satisfaction can depend very much on whether these questions can be answered affirmatively.

Thirdly, does the structure work managerially? Do the individual managers, such as department heads or chairs and faculty deans, have a reasonable number of people to line-manage? A typical management span of 5–20 people is reasonable. A much larger span would be unworkable, as the manager realistically would not be able effectively to support more than 20 staff reporting directly to him or her.

Fourthly, does the structure work in terms of the personalities and capabilities of the managers involved? This is a particularly complex issue and one which often gives rise to changes in structures being initiated.

Often, particular components in structures arise because particular academics champion and lead the development of wholly new degree disciplines or research areas. These academics then persuade more senior management to establish an appropriate department or unit. The senior academic involved then becomes the *de facto* head of that entity, but sometime later, it may be found that he or she is not a good manager or alternatively he or she may leave the institution. It then becomes necessary for senior management to replace the manager concerned.

In some cases, this may be easier said than done. Sometimes it is found that there are no natural successors within the university. Attempts to find a suitably qualified and experienced external replacement may also draw a blank. In cases like this, it may be more appropriate to alter the structure than leave the existing structure in place with inadequate management.

Structures can, therefore, be complex matters in universities that need careful management oversight. Senior managers need to ensure that the structures beneath

> **The structure needs to reflect the institution's academic character and ensure belonging and comradeship.**

them are effective and to take action if they are not. The structure needs to reflect the full academic character of the institution, ensure that both students and staff have a good sense of belonging and comradeship, and ensure that the managers in control of the various components in the structure are effective and good at their jobs. If any of these requirements are not met, it is incumbent on senior management to take appropriate action to improve the overall effectiveness of the institution.

Structural issues are not always easy to resolve as there is often simply neither an ideal structure for a particular university nor an ideal set of managers. The most senior managers, from the president or vice-chancellor downwards, have to do their best to make the structure the best they can at any one time. In some institutions this may result in frequent changes of structure, which should not be seen as a sign of weakness, but merely a sign that management is actively intervening to attempt to optimise organisational effectiveness.

Managing Institutional Ambition

Most universities are corporately ambitious and set themselves demanding targets in terms of size, status, national ranking, world ranking, etc. Although it may be regarded as somewhat surprising, many universities aspire to become "world-class". Evidence for this aspiration is found in the mission or vision statements of many universities, where the words "world-class" or "internationally outstanding" crop up with astonishing regularity.

Many universities seek to become global leaders and avidly chase the best academics as well as the best students to build their brand images.[19] Academia is thus intensely competitive at an international level, and most institutions aim to rise in status and recognition as time progresses.

Ambition, however, needs to be managed. Ambition may emerge from the will of the more senior academic staff of a university, from the president or vice-chancellor, or from the governing body, or perhaps from all of these collectively. Collective ambition feels good and can create a strong sense of purpose and hope, but it needs to be realistic as well as challenging. Unrealistic ambitions can demotivate staff or make senior management appear delusional. Thus, managers have an important role to play in defining the institutional ambition in a way that is meaningful to staff and seen to be achievable.

There is fundamentally nothing wrong in any university aspiring to be world-class. However, it has to be recognised that achieving such a status is an extremely long-term project. In his World Bank report on *The Challenge of Establishing World-Class Universities*,[20] Jamil Salmi identified three factors that define world-class institutions: (a) concentration of talent (academics and students),

(b) abundant resources to provide an outstanding learning environment and to support advanced research, and (c) appropriate governance.

Depending on the starting point, the journey may take several decades as a minimum and, for some that have achieved it, it has taken centuries. Becoming a global brand and attracting and retaining academics who are international superstars is very difficult to achieve.

Building the appropriate resource base, such as a substantial endowment, may also take a significant period of time, depending on the availability of donors and particularly contributions from alumni who have amassed substantial wealth over the course of their careers. Such donations may not pick up significantly until several decades after an institution has been established. In fact, it may take much longer than this in the early years because new institutions find it difficult to attract the very best students who are more likely to become richer and more inclined to donate to their alma mater late in life.

It is important to recognise that to achieve the standard and brand recognition of a top global university several things are required. To be distinguished internationally, a university must produce a large volume of world-class research and generate large numbers of publications arising from that research. To do that, a university must have the resources to hire top-class academics from around the world.

As academics are globally mobile, in order to attract them to an aspiring institution, they must be offered the conditions in which to build successful lives and careers. This means they need competitive salaries, academic freedom, the right to publish without restriction, access to good levels of government research funding, and the living environment in which to raise their families successfully (high-quality housing and schooling of outstanding international standard). These conditions are not easy to produce, especially in some developing or newly industrialised countries.

Depending on the age and standing of the university, the objective of becoming world-class is something that managers in a deeply aspirational institution must handle carefully. The outside world can easily see such high aspiration as unrealistically overambitious with the senior management in need of some recalibration of their thinking.

Yet, some institutions do make it to world-class status within a relatively short period of time. For example, a number have made it into the top 100 institutions in the various international league tables of universities within 50 years of foundation. Achieving this normally requires a continued focus on academic quality, and in particular on growing research and the quality of the top professors, over several generations of leadership. The ambition and vision have to be passed on from one president or vice-chancellor to the next many times over as well.

Moreover, the governing body—whose members may change over time—must adhere consistently to the same ambition. It is essential during such a journey that spending is prioritised on things that contribute to achieving the desired goal. This may include building up an outstanding library, providing state-of-the-art laboratories to support core science research centres, ensuring that staff have funds to travel to top international conferences, and last but not least, continuously working to upgrade the international standing of the academic staff by recruiting and promoting the best researchers and teachers. Only if such priorities are followed consistently through several decades can a relatively new institution begin to reach the upper levels of the international league tables.

Some Asian universities have managed to rise in global reputation and climb to very high levels in the global league tables within relatively short periods of time from their foundation. A good example is the Pohang University of Science and Technology (Postech) in South Korea founded in 1986. In 2011 it was ranked 28th in the Times Higher Education (THE) World University Rankings. This was an impressive position to hold after only 25 years of existence.

So, what enabled Postech to climb like this? Essentially the factors are similar to those that enabled Harvard University to grow in the 1950s and 1960s: the accumulation of a significant financial endowment (valued at around US$2 billion and provided by its parent company, the Pohang Iron and Steel Company) that enabled Postech to attract and reward top scholars, together with significant government support and research funding.[21]

Furthermore, Postech decided to use the California Institute of Technology (Caltech) as its role model, which at the time of writing, is ranked as the world's number 2 university in the THE ranking for 2020. Postech also kept its student recruitment highly selective and initially offered free places to most of its graduate students to attract top talent. Interestingly, however, it is pertinent to note that the challenge of maintaining a world-class ranking is considerable and by 2020, Postech had fallen to number 146 in the THE World University Ranking.

Along the way it is important not to create a "schizophrenic university", that is one with a split personality. Universities need to move towards the goal as a single entity. Sometimes attempts to move towards world-class status risk creating a university that has two personalities. This is a situation in which part, and only part, of the university is doing world-class work and is supported generously to do it. Meanwhile, another part is trying to become a more comprehensive institution, attracting a broad range of students and trying to fulfil the role of a general community-focused institution.

Trying to put two masks on one institution just does not work and can confuse stakeholders. This syndrome is especially likely to occur with newer universities that

> **It is important not to create a "schizophrenic university"; universities need to move towards their goal as a single entity.**

need to build their overall scale through appealing to the mass market of students, while at the same time, trying to build the world-class element in some of their academic departments. Creating split-personality institutions is something to be avoided as it can be difficult to tell a consistent message to staff, students, and the outside world. Everyone needs to know what kind of institution they are part of or are dealing with.

It is essential for senior managers and governors, in particular, to be vigilant about creating schizophrenic universities. It is relatively easy to do so if mixed priorities are laid down in institutional or divisional strategies. The institutional strategy must specify the direction of travel for the whole organisation and aspects which are conflicting or pointing in different directions need to be removed or resolved.

A typical example would be a strategy that calls for rapidly growing student numbers at the same time as growing the overall quality of research. Unless the student number growth strategy is managed well, it is likely to lead to the admission of weaker students and more hours in class for the academics, thus reducing their time spent on research.

The twin aims of growing student numbers and improving the quality of research need not necessarily be incompatible, but to avoid them becoming so, it is necessary for management to spell out how these two potentially conflicting aims are to be managed. Perhaps, for example, there will be a strategy to invest in new research posts as the revenue grows from the additional student volume. Whatever the answer is, it needs to be clear as the institution moves forward with its strategic plan.

Managing Rankings

Although many managers in universities would prefer to ignore them, the various national and international league tables (or rankings as they are also known) have become increasingly important and can have a significant effect on an institution's fortunes. Rankings are generated essentially using data analytics. League table positioning, either national or international, is an indication of the institution's quality and reputation and can influence the decision of some students, and particularly their parents, on whether to study there.

Rankings may also affect whether good academics choose to move to an institution and can also influence access to funding grants and chances of industrial collaborations. So, whether academic managers like them or not, they do have a bearing on an institution's fortunes and have to be taken seriously as a strategic issue.

As such, any university manager needs to be aware of where his or her institution currently stands in the league tables or ranking systems, and the factors that contribute to that positioning. Apart from ranking institutions overall, some league tables also rank universities in individual subject areas. Hence, deans and department heads or chairs may find that their own subject areas are being evaluated by the ranking organisations and put into subject league tables. Individual academic departments or faculties can thrive or decline as a result of this. So, presidents or vice-chancellors need to worry about their institutional ranking and deans and department heads or chairs need to worry about their subject rankings.

There is, of course, no such thing as a perfectly objective university-ranking system. This is one reason why many academics have a tendency to dismiss them. It is certainly true that journalists put more faith in them than is justified by the methodologies used to produce them. Nonetheless, journalistic interpretations do matter for university managers.

> **It is important for all academic managers to understand the factors that go into league table compilation.**

It is not uncommon for the media to demand government action when their national or local universities are seen to drop in the league tables. Though of course, the rankings are based on a range of factors that can fluctuate randomly year by year and short-term trends are not meaningful. Longer-term trends (5–10 years) may be meaningful and, if consistently in the wrong direction, require corrective action to limit reputational damage.

Most of the well-regarded international ranking systems rank fewer than the top 5% of higher education institutions. Therefore, to get a ranking, your institution has to be among the leaders worldwide by definition, otherwise it will simply not get any ranking and you will have no idea where your institution stands in comparison to others.

There are several global ranking systems for universities and the most prestigious ones are:

- Times Higher Education World University Rankings (THE): Using data analytics by Thomson Reuters, this highly respected ranking system assesses university performance in research, interaction with business, international outlook, and the teaching environment. The ranking is restricted to the top 1,400 institutions worldwide (effectively the top 5% currently).
- Academic Ranking of World Universities (ARWU): This was conducted originally by Shanghai Jiao Tong University but is now managed by a separate organisation, Shanghai Ranking Consultancy. The performance is judged principally on research such as the number of papers published in top journals and the number of staff with highly cited publications. The ranking was originally restricted to the top

500 institutions worldwide but has been expanded recently to the top 1,000.

- Quacquarelli Symonds World University Rankings (QS): This is mainly focused on the views of academic peers and employers from around the world, plus citation scores of published research papers analysed by Scopus. The ranking is restricted to the top 1,000 institutions worldwide.

Of lesser importance, but one which gives an alternative perspective of universities based on their websites is the Webometrics ranking system. This ranking system aims to rank all higher education institutions in the world and is conducted every six months by a Spanish organisation, The Cybermetrics Lab of the Spanish National Research Council. This ranking scheme is driven mainly by web presence including factors such as how many other organisations link to a university's website.

The major ranking systems (THE, ARWU, and QS) use research performance indicators as key factors in their rankings. Even the teaching factor in THE World University Rankings is focused on the teaching of research doctorates. In regard to research, the major factors which influence all of the major ranking systems are the number of research papers published in top international journals and the number of citations they receive (i.e., how many academics elsewhere cite the work of an institution's staff in their own publications). Even the Webometrics ranking uses citation measures from Google Scholar and assesses the number of other institutions' webpages that link to a particular university's website, which tends to indicate whether academics elsewhere find anything of interest on the website.

The overall message from this is that to rise in the ranking systems, a university must first and foremost increase the number of staff who undertake research which has a real impact on business or society, or transforms human understanding, and who then produce high-quality research papers that get cited by others. Apart from that, other actions that can improve the rankings would be to:

- increase the flow-through of visiting academics from other institutions (local and international) because of the peer opinion factor in the major rankings;
- increase the number of internationally recruited academics;
- increase the number of international students;
- improve the quality of material on the university's website;
- improve the staff-to-student ratio to the level of a major research-focused university (this is difficult to do for private institutions that rely mainly on student fees for their income and are not in receipt of significant government research funding); and
- increase the level of research grants and industry income received (this depends on the quality and abilities of the academic staff).

It may be thought that rising quickly in the international league tables is an almost impossible task. Yet many institutions, even relatively new ones, have been able to do it. The key for all managers involved in building reputation and rankings is to learn from those institutions that have been successful and to emulate the actions that have enabled them to grow and become more highly regarded. A range of strategies have been employed and much can be learnt from studying them and applying them at all levels of the institution.

As an academic manager, such as a department head or faculty dean, you should work out how to make your own department or faculty more significant in terms of ranking-related KPIs to help with the reputation-building of your institution overall. This is what would get you noticed as a successful university manager.

CHAPTER 13

Management and Governance

The Purpose of Governance

Although the emphasis of this book is on university management, it would not be appropriate to ignore governance, or more specifically, the way in which the institution's managers and its governing body relate to each other. The precise way in which the management and the governance functions interrelate can dictate the character of a university as well as its overall effectiveness. Good managers need to understand this and ensure that the management-governance interaction is a constructive one.

Most universities in the world have an overarching legal framework laid down by their national governments that specify how they are to be governed. Such a legal framework will also give universities the power to award their degrees that the government and employers will recognise. The overarching framework may be in the form of a charter, constitution, or any other such document. This legal framework will normally specify the governance structure.

In most universities, there will be a top-level governing body, board, or council. This will have overall responsibility for the strategic direction of the university, for its financial health, for its compliance with national regulatory requirements, for ensuring that it acts at all times in accordance with its charter or any other legal framework, for appointing and determining the remuneration of the senior officers, for its stability, and indirectly for its public profile and reputation.

Often, governing bodies establish subcommittees to oversee aspects of their work, such as finance, audit, and remuneration. Governing bodies normally delegate some of their powers to bodies within the university responsible for managerial control and academic control of the organisation (though still retaining ultimate responsibility).

Typically, there will be a top-level university management committee or executive committee that will oversee the effective management of the university. Such a committee comprises the senior managers of the institution. The committee will most likely have subsidiary committees responsible for particular areas of activity.

There will also typically be a top-level academic committee—often called the academic senate, court, or council—made up of the more senior academics, department chairs, deans, etc. It will also have subcommittees responsible for different areas of academic activity, such as teaching, research, quality procedures, library services, etc. The main function of an academic senate or similar body is to oversee the effective academic governance of the university. This may include determining the regulations around degrees, ensuring that effective academic quality procedures are operating, and determining the academic structure of the university, such as the number and names of faculties, departments, research units, etc.

Essentially, things that require academic-related decisions are normally delegated to an academic senate by the governing body. There is a very good reason for this. Most governing bodies are made up of external experts who are brought in, either on a voluntary basis or a paid basis, to guide the institution.

A typical governing body will have representatives from industry, local community organisations, government, educational institutions such as community colleges in the vicinity, as well as trustees of any charitable foundations that support the university, retired senior managers of other universities, and distinguished lawyers and accountants.

The governing body may have overarching legal responsibility for the university, but its members are essentially part-timers who attend a few meetings a year. They usually see their role as advisory, so long as they perceive that the management and academic governance structures beneath them are operating effectively. They usually have a wealth of managerial experience, but quite often not in academia. As such, governing bodies will not necessarily have the expertise or deep knowledge required for some of the more complex academic decision-making, which is why they rely on academic senates or similar bodies to undertake that role for them.

Although it is difficult to generalise at a global level, the tripartite model comprising the governing body, the university management committee, and the academic senate appears to be common to many, if not most, universities even though they may go under other names. The governing body sits at the top. Some institutions might also have a separate board of trustees who, for example, manage the funds or an endowment of the institution held in a charitable foundation.

The Management-Governing Body Relationship

The interplay within the tripartite system comprising the governing body, the university management committee, and the academic senate of a typical university is a complex one. The university president or vice-chancellor is normally the linchpin in this. He or she will normally chair a committee of senior university managers as well as the academic senate. He or she also needs to ensure that both of these act effectively. The president or vice-chancellor will normally also sit on the governing body as an *ex officio* member but does not control the governing body.

The president or vice-chancellor has to ensure that the wishes of the governors are understood, correctly interpreted, and passed on to the university management committee and to the senate. He or she also has to ensure that the governing body receives accurate information about the university's performance, which can then be used to inform their deliberations and judgements on key issues. More importantly, the president or vice-chancellor needs to ensure that the opinions, ideas, and concerns of the managers and the academics are communicated effectively to the governing body so that they do not make decisions in a vacuum.

Another key individual in the interaction between governance and management is the chair of the governing body. He or she needs to maintain a close relationship with the president or vice-chancellor and the two of them need to be in regular communication so that there is an ongoing dialogue about emerging issues.

In a strong, well-managed institution, there is a shared understanding of strategic direction and priorities between the governing body, the university management team, and the academic senate. All components of the tripartite system are pulling in the same direction. This utopian situation does exist in most universities, though not in all.

Normally, strategic plans will be drawn up by the senior officers of the institution and agreed by the university management committee after seeking views on the broad direction from the governors. The details of the plan will then be sent to the academic senate for consultation, perhaps also to student representative bodies, before being finalised by the university management committee and ultimately approved by the governing body. If that has been done well, everyone should be "on the same page".

> **All managers need to be aware of the importance of the interplay between the governing body, the university management, and the academic senate.**

All managers in universities need to be aware of the importance of the interplay between the governing body, the university management, and the academic senate or equivalent body and help to avoid the dysfunctions that can occur. This can often happen when the priorities of the governing body do not align with where the academic senate wants to go. Or perhaps more commonly, the situation arises in which the president or vice-chancellor wants to follow his or her own direction, paying little attention to the wishes of the academic senate or governing body. There are many real-life examples of where this has happened.

It is a fact that while governing bodies normally have ultimate responsibility for the success or failure of an institution, their influence over the course of events can be rather limited. They may lack detailed knowledge of what is going on, and there have been cases where universities have been found to have engaged in unsound or unwise activities with the governing body apparently unaware of what was really going on.

It is therefore important for all managers in universities to be aware of the tripartite nature of governance and management involving the governing body, the university management team, and academic senate,

> **Managers also need to understand their role in making the tripartite relationship work effectively.**

and of the role of the president or vice-chancellor in ensuring effective interaction between them. Managers need to understand their role in making this tripartite relationship work effectively in support of the president or vice-chancellor.

Misplaced Micromanagement

A situation that can cause major problems in universities is when members of the governing body try to interfere too much in institutional management. It is not uncommon to find that members of governing bodies are semi-retired individuals who enjoy their engagements with the university so much that they like to get involved in management decisions and effectively try to control the organisation themselves. This can result in key decisions being imposed on the president or vice-chancellor against his or her better judgement.

Given that the governing body has ultimate responsibility and can remove a president or vice-chancellor, there is not much the president or vice-chancellor can do if members of the governing body behave in this kind of way. Micromanagement is bad at any level in a university, and micromanagement by governors is particularly unwelcome because it often means that senior office holders, such as the president or vice-chancellor, provost, or deans, who are doing their best to keep multiple constituencies in harmony are effectively sidelined.

This can lead to rapid turnover of senior managers and problems lower down when decisions effectively taken by governors are imposed on academics without appropriate consultation through bodies such as the academic senate that the president or vice-chancellor chairs. Presidents or vice-chancellors, as well as their deputies and deans, need to be vigilant and try to deflect governor micromanagement.

This can be easier said than done, but pointing out that structures exist to take the key decisions and that governing bodies do not need to intervene unless they feel the institution is at risk can help. Good governing bodies will take the hint. Occasionally, however, governing bodies and presidents or vice-chancellors do fall out with each other, and that is often one of the primary causes of early termination of the president's or vice-chancellor's contract.[22]

CHAPTER 14

Managing Disruptive Changes

Disruption as Normality

No manager in a contemporary university can ignore the rapid changes in technology or fail to contemplate how what is now known as the Fourth Industrial Revolution[23] might impact on his or her institution. Some of these changes are likely to be disruptive to the way higher education is delivered and to the way universities operate in the future. No university leader wants to be seen as a Luddite, resisting inevitable changes.

Some pundits foresee the end of the traditional university campus as we know it with learners accessing high-quality course content online, including MOOCs, engaging with peers and professors via social media, and being assessed by artificial intelligence (AI) algorithms. While such technology-driven predictions of the end of the traditional campus may be premature, many higher education institutions now have to consider their future physical estates' needs in the context of increasing educational virtualisation.

Although MOOCs are often described as a disruptive technology that poses an existential threat to universities, the evidence so far is that they are mainly taken up by people who already possess degrees who use them to gain additional knowledge. They seem not to be replacing the experience of coming to campus to get a first degree.[24] Nonetheless, advanced technologies are undoubtedly changing the way higher education is being delivered and will continue to do so into the foreseeable future.

Disruption is likely to happen on many fronts, such as how education is delivered, who delivers it, where, and in what form. Traditional universities have not yet disappeared, but if young people can get necessary job skills by cheaply learning chunks of relevant knowledge from online sources, will traditional universities continue to exist long-term, at least as teaching institutions? Will there be a need for the state to provide higher education if private providers can package up and offer job-related learning very cost-effectively? These are issues that many managers in higher education will increasingly have to confront. Furthermore, some commentators even question whether current systems of education actually generate real value to students and society.[25]

Much of the recent growth in higher education provision globally has been primarily in the private sector, with private colleges and universities having been established to meet the demand for degrees from a growing aspirational middle class. Malaysia and India, for example, are two countries in which this trend of growing private higher education has been very evident with the same trend now occurring in Indonesia. Private higher education has been encouraged by governments anxious to raise tertiary education participation rates to

> **Disruption is likely to happen on many fronts, such as how education is delivered, who delivers it, where, and in what form.**

support and catalyse economic growth, but without drawing too heavily on very limited public funds.

Such institutions have teaching and learning as their primary focus and for most of them, research is a secondary or minor activity. Indeed, many receive little or no government research funding and find it difficult to justify using private student fees to pay for research activity, even though it may help to build the institution's academic culture and reputation as well as to attract good quality, academic staff.

Private institutions that have little research activity and whose purpose is mainly to provide education have no need for specialist research facilities. Without the need for research facilities, and with teaching and learning increasingly becoming virtualised in the online world, the question now arises as to whether a private higher education institution needs a campus at all.

Owners and directors of private institutions, especially in "for-profit" institutions, increasingly ask the question as to whether physical infrastructure and a cadre of full-time academic faculty are required at all in a commercial profit-maximising context. Some foresee the end of the traditional campus and see the potential to divest themselves of people and infrastructure, but still delivering high-quality education to their students. The fear exists that costs will be driven down by increasing virtualisation to such an extent that higher cost providers with significant infrastructure overheads will become uncompetitive and lose market share, and potentially go out of business.

So what, for example, is to become of private higher education institutions in the long term that have no desire, need, or support to undertake research? Will they move towards total virtualisation and move in the direction of becoming online institutions, or will they still see a need to retain a physical presence even in the face of rapid progress in technologies which could dramatically transform the way teaching, learning, and assessment are delivered?

AI could come to dominate higher education with students being advised by AI software and having their assessments, even sophisticated ones such as essays and technical reports, marked and given meaningful feedback by AI. However, the extent of this, and how soon it will happen, is still uncertain.

There is little doubt that this is now a period of immense change in society, and in higher education in particular, driven by technology. The impact of this change in higher education is most likely to be felt in the private sector, which is more sensitive to market forces and customer demands than the public sector. Institutions in the public sector are more insulated from rapid environmental changes through government subsidies, at least for research, and the need to preserve research infrastructure.

Fundamentally, private higher education institutions are likely to continue to play a very important and increasing role in educating the highly skilled workforce needed, in particular, in newly industrialising economies. The role of these institutions, however, will evolve to meet the expectations and requirements of their students. Learners will certainly want highly virtualised educational experiences and the flexibility that goes with this. Nonetheless, it is unlikely that this will lead to the death of the private higher education campus. The reasons for this are cultural and psychological.

> **Artificial intelligence (AI) could come to dominate higher education with students being taught, advised, assessed, and given meaningful feedback by AI.**

The whole way in which education is delivered is changing rapidly. Teaching has moved from the "sage on the stage",[26] to the "guide on the side", to the "star on the screen", and to the "friend on the app". This shift in who is involved in delivering education, where, and how is fundamental and will ensure that universities have to adapt to totally new ways of interacting with their customers. Young people may want the flexibility to study as and when they want in a virtual world and to be able to access high-quality content from anywhere to support their learning.

At the same time, young people also want real human contact. Any leader of a contemporary higher education institution will readily attest that groups of students hang around campus long after classes have finished to socialise and engage in social learning together. A campus provides the location for this to happen. It also provides the context in which young people learn to interact with each other as adults and to make friends and even find a future partner or spouse. Not much of this kind of activity can happen entirely in the online world.

Not only that, but most students do not want to remain at home separated from individuals of their own age apart from their siblings; nor do their parents want them at home all of the time, something that became apparent during lockdowns for the COVID-19 crisis. Universities and colleges, therefore, provide the meeting places, where group interactions can occur both for education and pleasure. Even in a highly virtualised educational context, the campus will remain a focus for young life, not simply a place to go and be educated in.

In some aspects, the campus of the future is more likely to resemble the classical Roman forum or Greek agora than a traditional campus full of teaching rooms, lecture theatres, and offices. It will be a place of socialisation, collective learning, and debate. It will still be a campus and will occupy an important place in the lives of young people.

The type of space it incorporates may evolve, but it will still be a campus, even if commercial pressures might suggest that universities of the future should dispense with them. University managers, therefore, need to think about what their campus will look like long-term, how they can adapt to new technological opportunities and ensure that their staff and resources are well optimised to take advantage of them.

Above all, universities are dynamic places which lead in the discovery and propagation of new knowledge. They are places that are likely to stimulate disruptive inventions and to challenge existing wisdom on many aspects of human life. In so doing, they are inextricably linked to the evolution of society. Managers in universities need to contemplate their role and always strive to be outstanding leaders in the way they do things.

The world needs universities that initiate, support, and respond well to disruptive changes. The world does not need universities that are locked into the status quo and unwilling to adapt to changes in their societies or to new ways of delivering their core missions. Good managers fully understand this and champion disruption, creativity, excellence, and inventiveness.

Besides changes in the *way* higher education is delivered, there are likely to be dramatic shifts in *what* is delivered. It is predicted that up to 50% of current jobs will be automated out of existence within 20 years, which means within half of the working life of today's graduates.

Graduates will therefore need the resilience to cope with a rapidly changing world in which their chosen professions may simply disappear. They may choose not to be educated in rigid single-subject degree programmes or in programmes that have any kind of "major" theme at all. They may find it far more useful and relevant to knit together a broad range of knowledge and skills picked up from different sources or institutions. Within their portfolio of skills, they will want traditional professional skills such as teamworking and business communication.

They may also want entrepreneurship skills, understanding of the power of the latest technologies, and knowledge of AI programming techniques. They may want accounting knowledge and legal knowledge to enable them to start businesses, even though their professional interest lies in the creative arts. All of these changes, and more, will drive fundamental changes in the way higher education is conceived, structured, offered, delivered, and consumed. Managers and leaders in contemporary higher education, therefore, need to be aware of the pace of change in higher education and recognise that disruptive influences are likely to come thick and fast. Disruptive change will be a normal aspect of managing a university for the foreseeable future.

Teamwork to Handle Disruptive Change

Given the demands of stakeholders in contemporary higher education and the need to lead institutions in such a way as to respond effectively to disruptive changes, managers need to ensure that they have supportive teams around them that can fully engage with disruption and assist in developing new ideas and in consulting staff more widely.

Change management is difficult to handle single-handedly. It needs a team of change agents who are all committed to making the changes necessary and who work towards a shared understanding of what needs to happen and then put in place a process to take other stakeholders, particularly staff, with them.

Managers in higher education who become isolated, or behave as though they personally have to drive the whole process of change on their own, are likely to be ineffective. This is because modern universities are such large complex organisations that one person rarely has an appreciation of the range of feelings among staff and students, or about the impact that disruptive changes are likely to have, both positive and negative.

> **Change management by teamwork is critical in universities in the context of highly intelligent potential naysayers.**

Change management by teamwork is critical in universities; arguably more so than in many other industries because academic leaders have to lead by demonstrating understanding and carefully considered rationality in the context of highly intelligent potential naysayers.

Managing Stress in Times of Change

This chapter would not be complete without addressing the issue of stress for managers and leaders in higher education, especially when driving disruptive institutional change. Being a manager or leader in a university can be a very rewarding role, but those that you lead can be very unforgiving if they feel you lack expertise, make bad decisions, or ignore the general sentiment of the "troops on the ground". Stress levels can soon rise if a manager becomes isolated and is seen to be ineffective in leading a team, especially when a major change is being introduced.

The key to keeping stress under control is not to drive change too fast, use EI as much as possible, and lead with a team that seeks consensus in charting a way forward. A manager who cannot do this is likely to have many sleepless nights and ultimately risks losing the confidence of his or her staff and eventually being replaced. In driving change, managers can also make the mistake of working too many hours every week and not taking adequate time for rest and reflection.

Excessively tired managers are often not effective and not able to engage in horizon-scanning and strategic contemplation. Too strong a focus on driving current change initiatives day in, day out can lead to preoccupation with minor issues and losing sight of bigger issues that are encroaching on the institution. Having sufficient rest and time for reflection and information gathering is essential in managing effectively in higher education. Great managers learn to manage themselves, and in particular their physical and mental well-being, as part of doing a great job of taking their institutions forward and embracing disruptive changes as opportunities.

CHAPTER 15
Growth as Your Leitmotif

Managers, individually and collectively, determine the success or failure of universities. Universities always want to be successful and need good management to be so.

In summing up the key messages of this book, a good understanding of key managerial concepts and the broader context of how universities function can enable a manager to grow within his or her job. An openness to learn and understand and, above all, to think about the strategic direction in which the university is headed will pay dividends, as will a focus on engaging with staff effectively and using EI as a team leader.

Ultimately, if you can look at the bigger picture, think strategically as well as operationally, and manage your part of the institution so that it fits with the organisation's overall strategy, you will find yourself highly appreciated and congratulated. Far too few university managers can do this. Far too many can only think about how to develop their own small part without looking at the bigger picture.

Many academic department heads or chairs will fight vigorously for extra resources for their area, at the expense of others. While this may make them very popular with their staff, this can cause problems for other departments and give managers above them a headache. Managers who can truly see things in an institution-wide way, consider the needs of the organisation as a whole, and balance that with the needs of their own area will succeed. The key is to ensure that your institution grows whether that be in terms of scale, quality, or reputation. As you help your institution grow, your own team grows and your own career can flourish. Growth is the underlying theme of what you do—it is the leitmotif to your daily academic life.

Good managers, who take a corporate view to managing, can see their careers blossom. Ultimately some of them will become great university leaders. Above all, being a manager in a university context can be hard as well as extremely rewarding. If this book has given you the confidence to deal with your responsibilities as a university manager and to feel that your job can be more enjoyable and rewarding because of that, it will have served its purpose.

List of Abbreviations

AI	Artificial Intelligence
ARWU	Academic Ranking of World Universities
EI	Emotional Intelligence
EQ	Emotional Quotient
HR	Human Resources
ICT	Information and Communications Technology
IQ	Intelligence Quotient
IT	Information Technology
KPI	Key Performance Indicator
MBWA	Management by Walking Around
MOOC	Massive Open Online Course
PR	Public Relations
QS	Quacquarelli Symonds
SLA	Service Level Agreement
SMART	Specific, Measurable, Achievable, Realistic, Timely
THE	Times Higher Education

Notes and Further Reading

1. Derek Bok, *Higher Education in America* (USA: Princeton University Press, 2013).

2. David Willetts, *A University Education* (UK: Oxford University Press, 2017).

3. John V. Lombardi, *How Universities Work* (USA: Johns Hopkins University Press, 2013).

4. Feng Da Hsuan, *Edu-Renaissance: Notes from a Globetrotting Higher Educator* (Singapore: World Scientific, 2016).

5. D. Quinn Mills, *Building World Class Universities in Asia* (CreateSpace Independent Publishing Platform, 2010).

6. John McCormack, Carol Propper, and Sarah Smith, "Herding Cats? Management and University Performance", *The Economic Journal* 124, no. 578 (2014): F534–F564.

7. Ken Blanchard, Donald Carew, and Eunice Parisi-Carew, *The One Minute Manager Builds High Performing Teams: Excellence Through Team Building*, 3rd New and Revised Edition (USA: William Morrow, 2009).

8. Marcus Buckingham and Ashley Goodall, *Nine Lies About Work: A Freethinking Leader's Guide to the Real World* (USA: Harvard Business Review Press, 2019).

9. David R. Caruso and Peter Salovey, *The Emotionally Intelligent Manager: How to Develop and Use the Four Key Emotional Skills of Leadership* (USA: Jossey-Bass, 2004).

10. William Oncken, Jr. and Donald L. Wass, "Management Time: Who's Got the Monkey?", *Harvard Business Review*, November–December 1999.

11. Alfons Van Marrewijk and Leonore Van den Ende, "Changing Academic Work Places: The Introduction of Open-Plan Offices in Universities", *Journal of Organisational Change Management* 31, no. 5 (2018): 1119–1137.

12. Cali Ressler and Jody Thompson, *Why Work Sucks and How to Fix It: The Results-Only Revolution* (USA: Penguin Books, 2011).

13. Jody Thompson and Cali Ressler, *Why Managing Sucks and How to Fix It: A Results-Only Guide to Taking Control of Work, Not People* (USA: John Wiley and Sons, 2013).

14. Larry C. Farrell, *The New Entrepreneurial Age: Awakening the Spirit of Enterprise in People, Companies & Countries* (USA: Brick Tower Press, 2001).

15. Clayton M. Christensen and Henry J. Eyring, *The Innovative University: Changing the DNA of Higher Education from the Inside Out* (USA: Jossey-Bass, 2011).

16. Burton R. Clark, *Creating Entrepreneurial Universities: Organizational Pathways of Transformation* (UK: Emerald Group Publishing, 1998).

17. Daniel Kahneman, *Thinking, Fast and Slow* (USA: Farrar, Straus, and Giroux, 2011).

18. Interestingly, although the COVID-19 pandemic has been seen as a major crisis for global higher education, it has also been viewed as an opportunity. See: Anthony C. Ogden, Bernhard Streitwieser, and Christof Van Mol, "How Covid19 Could Accelerate Opportunities for IHE", *University World News*, 4 April 2020, https://www.universityworldnews.com/post.php?story=20200403133447141.

19. Ben Wildavsky, *The Great Brain Race: How Global Universities Are Reshaping the World* (USA: Princeton University Press, 2012).

20. Jamil Salmi, *The Challenge of Establishing World-Class Universities: Directions in Development* (USA: The World Bank, 2009), https://openknowledge.worldbank.org/handle/10986/2600.

21. Philip G. Altbach and Jamil Salmi (Eds.), *The Road to Academic Excellence: The Making of World-Class Research Universities* (USA: The World Bank, 2011), https://openknowledge.worldbank.org/handle/10986/2357.

22. Stephen Joel Trachtenberg, Gerald B. Kauvar, and E. Grady Bogue, *Presidencies Derailed: Why University Leaders Fail and How to Prevent It* (USA: Johns Hopkins University Press, 2013).

23. Klaus Schwab, *The Fourth Industrial Revolution* (USA: Currency, 2017).

24. Jeffrey J. Selingo, *MOOC U: Who Is Getting the Most Out of Online Education and Why* (USA: Simon and Schuster, 2014).

25. Bryan Caplan, *The Case Against Education: Why the Education System Is a Waste of Time and Money* (USA: Princeton University Press, 2018).

26. Alison King, "*From Sage on the Stage to Guide on the Side*", *College Teaching* 41, no. 1 (1993): 30–35.

Acknowledgements

Firstly, I would like to thank the many university managers and leaders I have worked with closely for more than 20 years in senior management in higher education. Directly or indirectly, they have contributed to my own learning about university management. From most of them I have learnt many positive things. From one or two I have learnt, on occasions, how *not* to do things.

Both types of lessons are extremely valuable. In fact, I might even go as far as to say that the negative lessons have, on occasions, been the most important. Seeing when things go wrong, or watching other managers create new problems when trying to solve others, is extremely educational—or as one colleague once put it, "character building". I am grateful to them all.

Secondly, I would like to express my thanks to the outstanding team at Sunway University Press, led by Carol Wong, for bringing this book to fruition. I would also like to thank Professor Peter Heard, Provost of Sunway University, who has worked with me in senior management in two institutions and who has been an invaluable sounding board on how to get things right in university management. I would also like to thank him for his extremely helpful reflections on the material.

I would also like to thank Tan Sri Dato' Seri Dr Jeffrey Cheah, Chairman of the Sunway Group of companies, Malaysia, and the board of Sunway University for entrusting me with the enormous and humbling responsibility of leading the institution through a period of rapid change and expansion. The experience has undoubtedly taken my own understanding of academic and institutional leadership to a level that has enabled me to be able to write this book with maximum confidence.

Last but not least, I would like to thank my wife, Bo Li, who has experienced many good and bad managers in higher education. I am indebted to her for her wise and frank thoughts on the subject of university management.

Index

A

Academic Ranking of World
    Universities (ARWU),
    149–150
academic senate, 93, 136,
    154–160
academic stars, 59–64
academics
    entrepreneurial, 71
    research-focused, 40
    star, 9, 58
    talented, 55–56, 60
AI (artificial intelligence), 161,
    164–165, 168
alumni, 80, 82, 142
analytics
    data, 116–119, 121, 147, 149
    HR (human resources), 117
    marketing, 116
    research, 117
    social media, 117
    student performance, 116
appraisal, 88–89, 120
artificial intelligence. *See* AI

B

balance sheet, 114
behaviour
    bad, 26–27
    corrective, 28
    entrepreneurial, 70, 73
big data, 116
budget, 41, 54, 80, 85, 87–88,
    90, 114

C

Cabaret, 80
cats, 7, 12
charisma, 77

charter, 93, 136, 153–154
citation, 36, 114, 150
clean desk policies, 33
closure, 8, 68–69, 137
coach, 20, 26, 30
communication
    electronic, 97–100
    face-to-face, 99
    informal, 119
compensation, 60–61, 88, 107
conflict, 30, 37, 124
constitution, 92, 153
consultancy, 63–65, 82, 84, 114
control
    academic, 154
    cost, 90
    managerial, 154
    parental, 51
core mission, 76, 113, 167
coronavirus disease (COVID-19),
    130–131, 166
creativity, 41, 168
crisis, 10, 121, 129–133
cyberbullying, 101

D

delegation, 19–20, 24
diplomacy, 13, 53
disruption, 130, 162–163,
    168–169
disruptive change, 9, 167, 169,
    171
disruptive innovation, 8, 10
disruptive technology, 8, 162
diversity, managing, 49
dividends, 57, 172
donations, 82, 84, 89, 142
downwards, managing, 29

E

EI (emotional intelligence), 14–17, 20, 28, 30, 46, 53, 99, 133, 170, 172
electronic attacks, 101
email war, 100
emotional intelligence. *See* EI
emotional intelligence quotient. *See* EQ
emotions, 14–15, 17, 99–100
endowment, 81, 142, 144, 156
EQ (emotional intelligence quotient), 14–16
e-services, 108
executive summary, 103
expenditure, 81, 85–87, 89, 114
expertise, 42, 106, 156, 170

F

failure, 16–17, 59, 67, 87, 158, 172
fairness, 43, 51
feedback, 32, 36, 47, 56, 164–165
Fields Medal winners, 58
financial crisis, 2, 87, 89
flexibility, 12, 35–38, 63, 165–166
Fourth Industrial Revolution, 161

G

globalisation, 49
governance, 10, 93, 142, 153, 155, 157, 159
governance, articles of, 93, 136
governing body, 86, 93, 135–136, 141, 144, 153–160
growth, 2, 39, 67, 70, 111, 162–163, 173

H

headhunters, 60
hierarchy, 12, 29, 76, 121, 137
hierarchy of needs, 12

home, working from, 34–35
hot-desking, 33

I

income
    consultancy, 40, 86
    grant, 22, 40, 48
    research, 114
innovation, 3, 8, 41, 67, 70–71, 73
intellectual property. *See* IP
intelligence quotient. *See* IQ
interference, 63
international students, 2, 130, 151
interviews, 56–57
intrapreneurial, 68
IP (intellectual property), 82, 114
IQ (intelligence quotient), 14–16
Ivy League, 58

K

Kahneman, Daniel, 79
key performance indicators. *See* KPIs
knowledge transfer, 70, 106
KPIs (key performance indicators), 113, 115–118, 152

L

data protection laws, 53, 116
leadership, 10, 143
league tables, 143–144, 147–148, 151
learning
    blended, 32
    collective, 167
    social, 166
leitmotif, 173
Luddite, 161

M

management
    change, 169–170

emotional, 15
estate, 106
financial, 17, 90
risk, 120, 129
talent, 13
team, 29
management by walking around.
    See MBWA
management style
    consultative, 16
    emotionally intelligent, 16
managers
    charismatic, 77
    inexperienced, 30, 75
    new, 5, 73–76, 100
    support service, 107–110, 112
market share, 69, 164
Maslow, Abraham, 12
massive open online courses.
    See MOOCs
MBWA (management by walking
    around), 22
merger, 8, 68
micromanagement, 160
millennials, 51
monkey, 25–26, 30
MOOCs (massive open online
    courses), 8–9, 161–162

N

natural justice, 122, 125–128
negative publicity, 130
Nobel Laureate, 59, 79
Nobel Prize winners, 58
non-verbal cues, 99

O

objectives
    broad, 29
    financial, 81
    strategic, 11, 74, 115
    top-level institutional, 22

objectivity, 127
offices
    multi-occupancy, 33
    open-plan, 33, 41
outsourcing, 110

P

parents, 9, 32, 44, 51–53, 123,
    147, 166
partnership, 5, 107, 109
performance
    poor, 26–27
    research, 38, 117
    student, 116
personality tests, 60
Pohang University of Science
    and Technology (Postech),
    144–145
prejudices, 50
presentation, 41, 97, 103–104
pressure, 28, 51, 82, 123, 133, 167
privacy laws, 116
product, 3, 8, 40, 45–46, 67–68,
    71, 118
productivity, 36
promotion, 15–16, 77–78, 117
provost, 160

Q

Quacquarelli Symonds World
    University Rankings (QS),
    150
qualification, 1, 3, 45, 106

R

ranking systems, 38, 148–151
rankings, 48, 115, 135, 147–148,
    151–152
rational thinking, 132
recognition, 65, 78, 115, 141
recruitment, 32, 54–55, 57, 59
remuneration, 61–62, 154

research centres, 136, 144
research funding, 59, 145
research grants, 38, 43, 80, 84, 86, 89, 117, 151
research group, 59, 136–137
research institutes, 135
research paper, 34, 36, 38–39, 56, 114, 150–151
research units, 136, 155
resilience, 107, 168
revenue, 2, 70, 147
risks, managing, 10, 120, 129

S
Salmi, Jamil, 141
satisfaction
    customer, 45
    staff, 138
    student, 36, 41
schizophrenic university, 145–146
Scopus, 150
self-actualisation, 12, 19
service level agreement (SLA), 110
SMART approach, 21
social media, 32, 47–48, 69, 97, 117, 119, 133, 161
split-personality institutions, 146
status quo, 167
stress, 51, 63, 130, 132, 170
student dissatisfaction, 128
student numbers, 43, 69, 111, 146–147
student recruitment, 128, 145
student retention, 114
student unrest, 130
student voice, 46
students, managing, 9, 46, 49–50
subjectivity, 125
superstars, 58–60, 142
support services, 105–111
surplus, 81, 83, 85, 114

T
tact, 13, 53
taxation, 86
team
    academic, 26, 28
    crisis management, 132–133
    university management, 157, 159
teamwork, 170
tenure, 71
termination, 75, 160
Times Higher Education (THE), 144–145, 149–150
top talent, 61, 145
tripartite relationship, 159
tripartite system, 156–157
turnover, 85, 160

U
underperformers, 37–38
university management
    committee, 154, 156–158
upwards, managing, 29
U-turns, 127–128

V
vice-chancellor, 18, 29, 87, 123, 140–141, 148, 156–160
virtualisation, 161, 164
visibility, 6, 135
vision, 7, 17–19, 29–30, 87, 143
vision statement, 141

W
Webometrics, 3, 150
WhatsApp, 22, 31
workload, 25, 31, 42–43, 49
World Bank report, 141

BY THE SAME AUTHOR

Getting Promoted in Academia: Practical Career Guidance for Ambitious Academics and Aspiring Leaders in Higher Education

This short guide to career development for academics provides sensible and practical advice on how to rise to the top in the highly competitive world of higher education.

The book is packed with tactics and strategies for building a successful academic career and growing a strong personal brand as a leading and highly respected academic.

AVAILABLE IN PAPERBACK AND AS AN EBOOK